Frederick Bartlett Goddard

Grocers' Goods

A family guide to the purchase of flour, sugar, tea, coffee, spices, canned

goods, cigars, wines, and all other articles usually found in American

grocery stores

Frederick Bartlett Goddard

Grocers' Goods
A family guide to the purchase of flour, sugar, tea, coffee, spices, canned goods, cigars, wines, and all other articles usually found in American grocery stores

ISBN/EAN: 9783337329181

Printed in Europe, USA, Canada, Australia, Japan

Cover: Foto ©Lupo / pixelio.de

More available books at **www.hansebooks.com**

GROCER'S GOODS:
A Family Guide.

THE TRADESMAN'S PUBLISHING COMPANY,

Tribune Building,

NEW YORK CITY.

A FAMILY GUIDE

TO THE PURCHASE OF

FLOUR, SUGAR, TEA, COFFEE, SPICES, CANNED GOODS, CIGARS, WINES,

AND ALL OTHER ARTICLES

Usually Found in American Grocery Stores.

BY F. B. GODDARD.

THE TRADESMEN'S PUBLISHING COMPANY,

TRIBUNE BUILDING,

NEW YORK CITY.

Index List of Grocers' Goods.

Housekeepers will find this list suggestive and helpful in making up orders for the Grocer, as well as useful for page reference.

	PAGE.
Adulterations	6
Ale	62
Allspice	41
Almonds	50
Apples	44
Apples, Dried	48
Artificial Butter	30
Asparagus	47
Bacon	35
Baking Powders	16
Bananas	45
Barley	13
Bath Brick	58
Beans	47-48
Beef, Dried	35
Beef, Fresh	34
Beer	62
Berries	45-49
Beeswax	58
Bird Seed	57
Biscuit	16
Blacking	57
Blended Tea	24
Bluing	55
Brandies	63
Brazil Nuts	50
Bread	15
Brooms	56
Brushes	56
Buckwheat	14
Burgundy Wines	60-64
Butter	28
Butterine	30

	PAGE.
Cabbage	46
California Wines	61-64
Candies	19
Candles	55
Canned Goods	36
" Meats	37
" Fish	37
" Vegetables	38
" Fruits	38
Cans, Tin	38
Capers	43
Carrots	47
Cassia and Buds	41
Catsups	44
Cauliflower	47
Celery	47
Celery Salt	42
Cereals	10
Champagne	61
Cheese	31
Cherries	44
Chicory	27
Chocolate	27
Cider	63
Cigars	51
Cigarettes	52
Cinnamon	41
Claret Wines	60-64
Clothes Pins	56
Cloves	41
Cocoa	27
Cocoanuts	45
Cod Fish	35
Coffee	24

	PAGE.
Condensed Milk	28
Condiments	39
Cordials	64
Corn	12
Corn Starch	12
Crackers	16
Cranberries	45
Cream	28
Cream of Tarter	16
Cucumbers	47
Currants	45–49
Curry Powders	41
Dates	50
Disinfectants	58
Distilled Liquors	63
Dried Fruits	48
Eggs	33
Egg Plant	48
Essences	39
Extracts	39
Farinaceous Foods	14
Feed, for Stock	15
Figs	49
Filberts	50
Fish	35
Flavoring Extracts	39
Flour	11
Fruits	44
" Domestic	44
" Tropical	45
" Dried	48
" Brandy	39
" Canned:	39
Fruit Butter	39
Garlic	47
Gelatine	39
Gin	64
Ginger	40
Ginger Ale	63
Glucose	18
Gooseberries	45
Graham Flour	12
Grapes	44
Greens	48
Green Corn	47

	PAGE.
Groats	14
Grocers' Sundries	58
Halibut	53
Ham	35
Herbs	39
Herring	35
Hints to Housekeepers	8
Hominy	13
Honey	19
Horseradish	43
Insect Powder	58
Isinglass	39
Jams	39
Japan Tea	24
Jellies	38
Koumiss	28
Ketchup	44
Lager Beer	62
Lard	33
Lemons	45
Lentils	48
Madeira Wine	64
Maccaroni	17
Mackerel	35
Malt Liquors	62
Mace	41
Maple Sugar	18
" Syrup	18
Marmelades	39
Matches	57
Meal	12
Meat Extracts	36
Meats, Canned	37
" Fresh	34
" Smoked	35
Melons	48
Milk	9–28
Mineral Waters	61
Molasses	19
Mops	58
Mustard	40
Mutton	34

	Page.		Page.
Nuts	50	Salmon	35
Nutmegs	41	Salt	42
		Samp	13
Oatmeal	13	Sauces	43
Oil, Salad	43	Seeds	57
Olives	43	Shells	27
Oleomargarine	30	Sherry Wine	59-61
Onions	47	Shoe Dressing	57
		Snuff	53
Oranges	45	Soaps	53
Oyster Plant	48	" Toilet	54
		" Shaving	54
Pails	58	Soups Canned	37
Parsnips	47	Soda	16
Pea Nuts	50	Spaghetti	17
Peaches	44	Spices	39
" Dried	49	Squash	48
Pears	44	Starch, Laundry	55
Pearl Barley	13	Stove Polish	57
Peas	47-48	Stout	64
Pecan Nuts	50	Strawberries	45
Pepper	40	Sugar	17
Pepper, Cayenne	40	Sundries	58
Pepper Sauce	44	Sweet Potatoes	46
Pickles	43	Syrups	19
Pipes	51		
Pine Apples	45	Tamarinds	50
Plums	44-49	Tapioca	15
Pork	34	Tea	21
Porter	62	Tobacco, Chewing	51
Port Wine	59-61	" Smoking	51
Potatoes	46	Tomatoes	47
Poultry	34	Tongues	35
Preserves	38	Turnips	47
Prunes	49		
		Veal	34
Radishes	47	Vegetables, Fresh	46
Raisins	49	" Canned	38
Rice	14	Vermicelli	17
Rhine Wines	60-64	Vinegar	42
Rhubarb	47		
Rum	64	Washboards	46
Rye Flour	13	Wines and Liquors	59
		Wheat	10
Sago	15	Whiskey	64
Salads	48		
Salad Dressings	43	Yeast	16
Saleratus	16		

GROCERS' GOODS.

A FAMILY GUIDE.

In the ancient times of twenty-five or thirty years ago, the grocer's goods consisted chiefly of codfish, flour, sugar, tea, coffee, salt, molases and whale oil. There were also a little candy in glass jars, some nuts in bins, a few drums of figs and a box of sour oranges. The grocer himself found plenty of time to talk politics and play checkers across the counter with his friends and neighbors. Those were the days when a few conservative old merchants used to meet and discuss the tea market and allot among themselves the quantity to be imported, not a pound of which could arrive under twelve or fifteen months.

But things have changed. The importer now flashes his order under the sea and on, over plains and through jungles to China. "Ocean tramp" steamships are waiting to receive his merchandise, and within thirty or forty days it may be sending up its grateful fragrance from tea tables in the Mississippi Valley.

THE MODERN GROCER.

Nor has the enterprising retail grocer of to-day failed to catch the spirit of this progress and keep even step with it. He has become the Popular Food Provider, and his store represents about everything which is palatable in either hemisphere or any zone. As the world has grown enlightened and refined, his stock has become more and more varied and better adapted to the wants of mankind, until it embraces every delicacy of the land, sea or air.

His cunningly prepared sauces provoke the appetite and give zest to more substantial articles, while they help also to digest them. He has food fitted for the intellectual worker and for the laborer, for the invalid and for the infant. He practically annihilates the seasons and furnishes fruits and vegetables in mid-winter, as fresh and delicate as when first plucked from their native stems or vines. And, moreover, all the goods upon his sightly shelves are now put up in the most attractive, portable and convenient form for family use.

Food Never Before so Low.

Nor would a day's wages ever before purchase so much of food products. In the English market, for the ten years from 1870 to 1880, the price of wheat was forty-three per cent. higher than the average of 1886. Sugars have fallen in price nearly one-half in ten years, and teas, coffee, and many other articles are proportionately low.

This is due to improvements in machinery, increased transportation facilities and the opening up of new and fertile sections of the earth, under all of which the world's supply of food has of late years been greatly in excess of the world's increase in population; and it is the grocer who brings these advantages home to our families.

Food Adulteration.

There has long been an uneasy feeling lest many articles of food and drink were not only mixed with substances which reduced their nutritive value, but were also often colored with cumulative poisons, and adulterated with substances injurious to health.

These fears have not been altogether groundless. There can be no doubt that this monstrous crime has been practiced to some extent in respect to certain articles. But, thanks to the diffusion of intelligence, the teachings of science, the operation of law, the fear of detection and punishment, and largely, also, by the refusal of conscientious grocers to sell such unwholesome products; greedy and unscrupulous manufacturers have been compelled to abandon their vicious practices, and noxious food adulteration is now comparatively a rare crime.

Those who desire pure articles can almost always obtain them of a reputable grocer by paying their value. But in order to supply the demand for cheaper goods and meet competition, such articles as powdered spices, etc., are extensively prepared, mixed with harmless substances, and containing the largest quantity of pure material which can be furnished at the price for which they are sold. Perhaps, also, such articles are more economical in the using, and admixtures are sometimes improvements.

Adulteration Laws.

Yet even this class of adulterated goods is objectionable, from the fact that there are always dealers who will be tempted to sell them as "Strictly pure," thus defrauding the purchaser, out-reaching honest rivals and losing their own self-respect. Probably, therefore, most of the upright and leading grocers of the country would be glad to see wise and effective general laws passed against food adulterations, under which all could unite and be freed from unfair competition by the unscrupulous. But laws which will protect both the health and the pocket are difficult to frame and to execute without being sumptuary and oppressive. The most effectual and probably the best laws of the kind in this country at present are the enactments of Massachusetts, New York, Ohio, New Jersey, and Michigan.

Less Adulteration than Commonly Supposed.

The general Government is also moving in the matter. Last year (1887) three "Bulletins" were issued at Washington, which deal exhaustively with current adulterations of dairy products, spices, etc., and fermented beverages. These reports, made under direction of the Commissioner of Agriculture, were prepared respectively by Messrs. H. W. Wiley, C. Richardson, and C. A. Crampton, who state in substance that they found certain articles extensively adulterated, but generally with harmless materials.

The president of the N. Y. Microscopical Society states that many members of that scientific body have looked into the alleged adulterations of food products and find them not as general as many suppose, and the adulterants found were in most cases harmless.

At the recent "Health Exhibition," in England, Dr. Jas. Bell declared to the Conference, that, "In most articles of food there has been a very great improvement in recent years as regards

adulterations," and that the "gross and deleterious adulterants
formerly used have been practically abandoned." This accords
also with the recently expressed opinions of the eminent Dr. Has-
sall and of many scientific investigators in this country.

Hints to Housekeepers.

As a rule, whole or unground articles are to be preferred to
those which are powdered; not only because they are less liable
to adulteration, but also because the latter more quickly lose
flavor and strength.

This objection applies also to buying goods in large quantities
of wholesale dealers, for family use. This plan may appear to be
economical, but is generally disadvantageous both to buyer and
seller. Tea, aromatic and ground goods, and many other com-
modities often deteriorate in quality before they are used. Ser-
vants who can dip their hands into abundant supplies are apt to
become more wasteful. If articles so purchased do not prove
suitable, it is more trouble to exchange them than with the retail
dealer who sells in smaller quantities and is in daily contact with
his customers. And, besides, an honest man who studies the
daily wants of the families of his community, and adapts his
business to supplying them with good articles in convenient
quantities and at fair prices, has a right to expect consideration
and encouragement from his friends and neighbors.

The Daily Food of a Model Man.

A healthy man, weighing, say, one hundred and fifty-four
pounds, consists of water one hundred and nine pounds, and of
solid matter forty-five pounds. His blood weighs about twelve
pounds, or, when dry, two pounds. The quantity of food substances he should consume every day, and their relative proportions necessary to keep him vigorous and well, are stated by
Prof. Johnston to be about as follows:

	lbs.	oz.
Water	5	8¼
Albumen, fibrin, gluten, etc.		4¼
Starch, sugar, etc.		11½
Fat		3¼
Common salt		¾
Phosphates, potash salts, etc.		½

If for a time the proper balance of constituents is not preserved in the food, even though the health may not appear affected, the laborer can do less work, a frail constitution is engendered and the person becomes more susceptible to disease.

Variety in Food.

If any constituent is deficient we must supply it; hence variety in food is not only agreeable but necessary to health. Albumen, fibrin, casein and gluten build up the muscles and tissues, while starch, sugar and fat produce the warmth and energy of the body. The mineral substances are necessary for the framework—the bones. Grains, fruits and vegetables contain starch and sugar and more or less gluten; meats contain fibrin and albumen; milk, casein, etc.

Beef and Bread

have the following composition:

	Lean beef.	Wheaten Bread.
Water	77	40
Fibrin or gluten	19	7
Fat	3	1
Starch	0	50
Salt and other minerals	1	2
	100	100

This shows that the main difference between beef and bread is that the meat contains no starch, and nearly three times as much of the muscle making fibrin as the proportion of gluten (which is similar in many respects) in wheaten bread.

The water, climate, season, age, habits, etc., all have to do with the choice of food we eat. Besides the quantity of nourishment contained in the food, there is also the question of the ease and completeness with which it can be digested and assimilated. It is not always fat eaters who are the fattest.

Milk.

Woman's milk is considered the type of human food when the conditions approach that of the child, as the milk of the mother is the natural food of all young animals. Milk partakes of the nature of both animal and vegetable food. It contains:

	Human milk.	Cow's milk.
Water...	89½	87
Casein..	1⅜	4
Butter or milk fat....	2¼	3¼
Sugar of milk...........	6⅛	4¾
Salts or ash...................... ..	¼	¾
	100	100

These are average analyses. The casein is equivalent to the gluten of vegetables or the fibrin of meat, and the sugar to starch.

With these few general observations, let us pass on to consider in detail the Grocer's Goods.

THE CEREALS.

WHEAT.

The cereal grains consist of solidified vegetable milk, drawn from the bosom of Mother Earth. But two of them all are used for making light and spongy bread with yeast, and wheat has the universal preference because it contains all the elements necessary to the growth and sustenance of the body. It makes bread which is more inviting to the eye and more agreeable to the taste. It is the highest type of vegetable food known to mankind, and it is claimed that the most enlightened nations of modern times owe their mental and bodily superiority to this great and beneficent product.

There is little if any difference in the nutriment or value of spring and winter wheat. Some prefer the one and some the other. Southern raised wheat is apt to be drier than northern and will better stand the effects of warm climates. Wheat varies in weight per bushel as the season is wet or dry. The best is round, plump and smooth. It contains about fifteen parts of water, sixty-five to seventy-five parts of starch, and about ten parts of gluten. The average annual production of wheat in the United States during the past eight years has been 448,815,699 bushels; an increase over the preceding ten years of forty-four per cent., while the increase of population has been only twenty-five per cent.

Wheaten Flour.

Wheat was formerly ground by mill stones, and the product bolted and sifted into the different grades. But during the last twelve years, this process has been largely superseded by the "Patent Roller" process of crushing and separating the flour from the bran. This is a great improvement over the old method; more flour is obtained from the wheat, and it is whiter, contains more gluten, and is therefore stronger

The first consideration is the color or whiteness; second, the quantity of gluten the flour contains. The eye determines the first, and a hasty test of the quantity and quality of the gluten may be made by squeezing some of the flour into a lump in the hand. This lump will more closely show the prints of the fingers, and will hold its form in handling with considerable more tenacity if the flour is good, than if it is inferior and deficient in gluten.

Grocers and bakers test flour by smoothing a little out on a board with a knife or paper cutter, to see its color, and if it contains specks of bran, etc., which may show that it has not been well bolted or "dressed." To determine the quantity and strength of the gluten, they mix some of the flour with water, and judge by the tenacity of the dough—the length to which it may be drawn out by the fingers, or spread into a thin sheet.

Injury to flour is shown most quickly in the gluten, which may lose its vitality. The gluten of good flour will swell to several times its bulk under a gentle heat, and give off the pleasant odor of hot bread, while the gluten from poor flour swells but little, becomes viscous or nearly fluid, and smells disagreeably.

Points for Purchasers of Flour.

As starch is whiter than gluten, whiteness is therefore really no indication of the sweetness and strength of flour; and, although flour becomes whiter with age and will take up more water and make a whiter loaf, many prefer freshly ground flour for family use, as being better in flavor, while others claim that flour will "work better " if kept for some time after grinding.

The brand or word "Patent" on packages of flour has come to signify, not that the flour is really patented, but that it is or should be finest quality. Fancy brands may mean little; they are put on at the whim of the maker. Flour is rarely adulterated at present, but good and poor grades are sometimes mixed. Inferior grades of flour are largely exported, while the best are mainly used at home. Graham flour is ground wheat from which the bran has not been removed.

Flour is put up in barrels of one hundred and ninety-six pounds net weight, and in muslin sacks of various weights. Families everywhere invariably want "the best," and dealers often adopt the excellent plan of buying quantities of some very choice and tried grade of flour and selling it in convenient sized packages for family trade, under their own brand and guarantee.

Corn or Maize.

This is one of the most beautiful of plants, and the Indians formerly ascribed to it a Divine origin. Hiawatha watched by the grave of the Spirit Mondamin,

> " 'Till at length a small green feather
> From the earth shot slowly upward,
> Then another and another,
> And before the summer ended
> Stood the maize in all its beauty,
> With its shining robes about it,
> And its long, soft, yellow tresses."

Indian corn contains more oil or fat than any of the common cereals. It will make as white and fine flour as wheat, but this does not make good fermented bread, unless mixed with wheaten flour. CORN MEAL is healthful, nutritious and cheap, but, owing to its fat, is prone to attract oxygen and spoil, especially in warm weather. There are two kinds, one WHITE, the other GOLDEN YELLOW. They are equally nutritious, and about the same in price. Some prefer the one and some the other, but probably the yellow is rather the most popular. The starch extracted from corn is very extensively used throughout the country, and such leading brands of CORN STARCH as those of Kingsford, Duryea, etc., are well known. In fact, the consumption of all the products of corn is enormous.

SAMP is corn deprived of its skin and eye and left whole or cracked in halves. HOMINY is corn ground or cracked into coarse, medium or fine grains, and pearled or polished. DRIED CORN, largely prepared by the Shakers, is sweet corn boiled and dried. It is excellent and much used as a vegetable.

Rye Flour.

Rye ranks next to wheat for bread making, and is equally nutritious. It yields less flour and more bran than wheat, contains more sugar, and is darker in color. Its gluten has less tenacity and it will not make as light and spongy bread as wheat flour, hence is little used in this country. Rye flour should contain a little of the bran, as this has a pleasant, aromatic flavor. The "Black bread," so extensively eaten in portions of Europe, is made of rye flour. It is dark, heavy and sourish, but like all rye bread, has the property of keeping moist a long time. Two parts of wheat with one of rye flour makes wholesome and palatable bread.

Barley.

This grain is less nutritious and less digestible than wheat, but contains more sugar and more of the phosphates, and is also cooling. It will not make good bread, but is sometimes used for the purpose, mixed with wheaten flour.

PEARL BARLEY is the whole grain freed from its hulls like rice. It is used in soups, etc., and is sold by all grocers. In the best qualities the grains are large and well rounded. It is sold in bulk and in pound packages.

Oatmeal.

Oats are substantial, nutritious and wholesome, being rich in gluten and fat. Oatmeal for the table is made from kiln dried, large, white oats, freed from the husks. Alone it does not make good bread. If long used as a sole or chief food it is reputed to overtax the digestive organs, heat the blood, and produce eruptions of the skin. Many claim, however, that these effects are due solely to insufficient cooking of the meal or porridge, and there are excellent preparations in market which have been well cooked by steam and afterwards dried.

Besides these there are various brands of Scotch, Irish, Canadian and American oatmeal, "Crushed," "Rolled," "Granulated," etc., also oat "AVENA," "FARINA," etc. GROATS are the whole kernels of oats deprived of their husks. The consumption of oatmeal has vastly increased within five or six years, and is rapidly becoming universal. Salt only *after* cooking. If added before, salt tends to harden the meal and prevent its swelling.

Buckwheat.

This grain may be classed with wheat as regards its nutritive qualities. It contains thirteen or fourteen per cent. of water, about fifteen per cent. of gluten, and sixty or sixty-five per cent. of starch. It will not make good fermented bread, but its delicious cakes are an essential and attractive feature upon American breakfast tables everywhere, especially in cool weather. It is sold in bulk and is also put up in three and six pound packages.

Rice.

Although this grain is the main food of one-third of the human race and is very easily digested, it contains too little gluten and fat and too much starch to be considered alone as a perfect food for man. Rice has a slightly constipating effect but is an excellent and wholesome occasional article of diet, and one which could not well be spared from the family list. Rice is sold deprived of its husk. It is imported from the East Indies, but the best is the fine, large head rice of the Carolinas. As some of the most valuable qualities of rice dissolve out in hot water, it should be steamed until tender, rather than boiled.

Farinaceous Foods.

These are very numerous and some of them are excellent. Among them may be named the "CEREALINE FLAKES," made from white corn; CRACKED and CRUSHED WHEAT, WHEATEN GRITS, FARINA, which is the inner part of the wheat granulated, SELF-RAISING BUCKWHEAT and other FLOURS; "WHEATLET," "GRAIN-LET," "GRANUM," "FARINOSE," "MAIZENA," MANIOCA, INFANT

FOOD, MILK FOOD, ARROW ROOT, CORN STARCH of various makes, GRAHAM FLOUR, BOSTON BROWN BREAD MIXTURES, etc. Many of these preparations are eaten with milk, and prove valuable additions to the family diet.

SAGO is the pith of an Indian palm steeped in water until it becomes a paste, then formed into little balls by rubbing it through a perforated plate. The best is the whitest. TAPIOCA is the pith of the Manihot tree, washed like sago, but granulated differently. Both are nutritious and easily digested, and are made into puddings, often with fruit, and eaten with milk or sauce.

Bread.

One hundred pounds of good, fine, wheaten flour will take up forty-five pounds of water, and yield one hundred and forty-five pounds of bread. The proper and legal weight of bread is while it is hot. A four pound loaf loses in twenty-four hours one and one-quarter ounces; in forty-eight hours five ounces; in seventy hours nine ounces. The quantity of water which flour will absorb depends largely on the proportion and quality of the gluten. The best flours absorb most, and will take up more in dry than in wet seasons; hence a dry season is good for the baker. Thorough kneading increases the absorption of water, and should be continued until none of the dough will stick to the hand.

Feed for Stock.

Among the articles largely used as food for animals are the refuse products of the various grains made in preparing them for human consumption; as, for instance, the refuse left in the pearling of barley, or in making hominy and samp; dried BARLEY SPROUTS from malt, low grade flour; MIDDLINGS, which are a mixture of bran and flour; BRAN, etc. Besides these, OATS, white, black and mixed, and vast quantities of Southern and Western CORN are also used for stock, ground into coarse meal.

Bread Raising Materials.

Fermentation, says Liebig, is not only the simplest and best, but likewise the most economical way of making light and porous bread.

YEAST is a true fungous plant, which has the power of establishing fermentation and changing starch into sugar, and the escaping gas makes the loaf light and spongy. -- Hops prevent too great fermentation and impart an agreeable flavor. BREWERS' YEAST is largely used when obtainable, and there are many domestic modes of preparing yeast from potatoes, flour, etc.

DRIED YEAST.—But as all these fresh yeasts are liable to spoil and affect the bread unpleasantly, there is an extensive demand for a yeast which shall possess the same properties and which may be kept a long time. Hence, the various brands of yeast cakes sold by the grocer. They are made usually by adding corn meal to the yeast and carefully drying the cakes in the sun. It is singular that a fall or sudden jar may injure yeast cakes and deprive them largely of their qualities.

CREAM OF TARTAR, BI-CARBONATE OF SODA, BI-CARBONATE OF POTASH (SALERATUS), are all used in bread making, and are to be had in all sorts of packages of the grocer. Cream of tartar is tartrate of potash, and is made from the argols found incrusted upon the inside of wine barrels. It should be white, and not yellowish in tint. The effect of these chemicals in raising bread is due chiefly to the liberation of the carbonic acid gas they contain when mixed with water, incorporated with the dough and put in the oven, and the great requisite is that they should be pure and unadulterated.

BAKING POWDERS are much used for making light and palatable domestic biscuits, etc. They are convenient, and generally lessen the quantity of shortening required. They are made chiefly of tartaric acid and bi-carbonate of soda, and should be neutral to the taste, and without effervescence if either an acid or alkali is added. One popular variety, called "Phosphatic Baking Powder," consists of acid phosphate of lime instead of cream of tartar, with soda.

Biscuits, Crackers, etc.

The word biscuit means twice baked, and is a survival from the ancient mode of cooking the cakes which is now no longer in use. Plain biscuits are said to be more nutritious than bread in the proportion of five to three, and are most digestible when light and well browned in baking, so as to turn much of the starch into dextrine. Sea biscuit or ship bread is made simply of flour and water baked at a high heat. In the large cracker bakeries the dough is mixed, rolled and cut by machinery and the cakes travel on through patent ovens until baked, when they drop out into baskets. Those made by hand are, however, considered best.

The variety of biscuits and crackers in market is utterly bewildering. These are among the standards: BOSTON, SODA, BUTTER, OYSTER, SUGAR, FRUIT, MILK, ENGLISH ALBERT, WATER, CREAM, GINGER, LEMON, OATMEAL, CARAWAY, VANILLA, and dozens more kinds of biscuits, crackers and wafers at various prices; besides GINGER and LEMON SNAPS and JUMBLES, and even DOG BISCUIT. There is also CRACKER DUST, for frying oysters, fish, etc. Some of the above come in handsome tin packages.

MACCARONI, VERMICILLI, SPAGHETTI.—These are all made from the dough of the hardest and most glutenous Southern wheat, and the domestic are inferior to the Italian or French. The best will merely swell and soften after long boiling, and still retain its form. Maccaroni is in small tubes, spaghetti in small stems, and vermicelli in threads or shreds. Letters, stars, and other figures are also made from the same material or paste; all are largely used in soups. EGG NOODLES are ribbon maccaroni.

SUGAR AND THE SWEETS.

This necessity of modern life ranks as one of the most important articles among the grocers' goods. Two hundred years ago it was sold chiefly by the apothecaries, but is now consumed in all parts of the world to the extent of many millions of tons annually. Sugars have been divided into four kinds, viz.: cane sugar, found in stems; grape sugar, found in fruits; manna sugar, found in leaves; and milk or animal sugar.

There are many varieties of the sugar cane which contain from twelve to twenty per cent. of sugar; these are cut, crushed, and the juice boiled down and clarified with lime, etc.; the sugar crystallizes and leaves the molasses. The sugar beet contains from seven to thirteen per cent. of sugar, which, when raw, is unpleasant, but when refined is identical with cane sugar. The fact that the molasses of the sugar beet, although colorless, is very disagreeble, has retarded the beet sugar manufacture, but it is a great and growing industry. The sap of the sugar maple contains about two per cent. of MAPLE SUGAR, which is identical with cane sugar, and may be made white, but is preferred brown, as containing more of the rich maple flavor. About seven thousand tons of maple sugar are annually made in the New England States. MAPLE SYRUP is extensively sold by grocers in cans, bottles, etc.

GRAPE SUGAR OR GLUCOSE.—The sweetness of ripe fruits is due to the starch which they contain, passing, under the ripening influence of nature, into grape sugar. Substances may consist of the same elements, but different proportions may greatly vary their properties. For instance, starch and sugar consist merely of carbon and water. Grape sugar contains more water than starch, and cane sugar more than grape sugar.

Now, long boiling of starch in pure water produces little change upon it; but it was found that if a little sulphuric acid is added, the starch will take up more water and become entirely converted into grape sugar. And this is substantially the way in which commercial glucose is made. The acid is neutralized by lime, and the liquor boiled down into solid grape sugar or syrup.

CANE SUGARS are sweeter than grape sugars in the proportion of five to three; hence, three pounds of cane sugar are worth five pounds of grape or starch sugar for sweetening purposes. This is the reason why grape sugar is used to adulterate cane sugar, and it is the only adulterant used at present to any extent.

One pound of water will dissolve three pounds of cane, but only one pound of grape sugar. The latter has a gummy taste on the tongue and dissolves slowly. A small grained sugar may carry some glucose and perhaps escape detection, but the crystals of a large grained sugar will always be brilliant in contrast with its contaminating ingredients, and thus proclaim the fraud. In other words, inferior sugars have a dull look, while good sugars are bright. Glucose sugars melt at one hundred and five degrees,

C., while cane sugars melt only when heated to one hundred and thirty-seven degrees, C. Raw sugars are no longer used. They should be refined to free them from the repulsive sugar mite and other impurities. The best sugar is always the most economical.

THE BEST GRADES OF FAMILY SUGAR are the cut loaf, cubes and crushed. Next in market value, in the order in which they stand, are powdered, granulated, A sugars, C sugars, white, yellow, extra golden, etc., down to common yellow.

SYRUPS.—These are the uncrystallized residue in refining brown sugars. They are diluted, filtered through animal charcoal, and concentrated. The lighter the color the higher the price. The better qualities are called "Rock Candy Drips," "Golden Drips," etc.

MOLASSES.—The choicest are the New Orleans Fancy, Choice, Prime. Good, etc., down through the same grades of Porto Rico, to the Cuba Muscovado. The quality of molasses has deteriorated with improvements in the manufacture of sugar on plantations, and it is sometimes sold mixed with glucose.

HONEY.—Consists of eighty parts in a hundred of pure grape sugar with an acid and aromatic principle. Spring honey is better than that made in autumn, and that from clover or other fragrant flowers is better than that of buckwheat.

Sugar Candies.

Whatever dangers may have lurked in confectionery in times past, parents may now be assured that they can gratify the natural and healthy appetite of their children for sweets, without fear of poisonous colorings or harmful adulterants.

The "National Confectioners' Association," (an organization formed by a large proportion of the leading manufacturing confectioners of the United States,) "is pledged by its constitution and by-laws to prosecute all parties using poisonous colorings, terra-alba, or other mineral substances in the manufacture of confectionery." They invite fathers and others interested to report any supposed case of injury from eating poisoned candy, and "offer a reward of one hundred dollars for evidence that will en-

able them to convict the offender." It is the opinion of the
editor of the *Weekly Confectioner*, and of many prominent manufacturing confectioners in New York, as expressed to us, that in
all the land there is now no product of domestic manufacture and
consumption which is more free from poisonous colorings and injurious adulterants than confectionery.

But more than this: in 1886 this association passed an amend-
ment to its constitution forbidding any member, under penalty of
expulsion, to buy or sell "any candy adulterated with flour, corn
meal, starch, or cerealine, except such amount of starch as is
necessary to the manufacture of gum goods and fig paste work."
Many confectioners, however, think this action was ill advised.

Making Candy, etc.

Glucose or grape sugar now enters largely into the manufacture
of many kinds of confectionery, and harmless vegetable colors
are used.   Manipulation breaks up the crystals of sugar and
thereby renders it whiter, and the difference in the price of candies is now largely due to the amount of manipulation it receives.
Few have an idea of the vast quantities of confectionery manufactured.   It amounts to many hundred tons daily; much of it is
made almost entirely by machinery, and the business is divided.
For instance, one firm makes only lozenges, another gum drops,
caramels or licorice, marshmellow, etc.   Jobbers supply re-
tailers.

If synthetic or chemically prepared flavoring extracts are used,
they are such only as are guaranteed harmless.

French imported "Bon Bons" are still superior to the domestic, and so are their candied violets; but rose leaves iced here
are equal to the imported.   Licorice candies are having an increased demand yearly.   Cocoanut candy contains usually a large
admixture of the harmless cerealine.   Space will not permit
more than a reference to the great variety of confections in market.   Among them are stick and lump candies in scallops and
patties, with mottoes, etc., assorted and in various colors; mixed
candies in various forms and flavors, gum drops, lozenges, white,
red and assorted; rock candies, etc.

FAMILY BEVERAGES.

TEA.

This staple necessity of modern life is now consumed by more than five hundred millions of people, and its use appears to grow with the growth of civilization. There is but one species of the tea plant and its varieties are due to differences of soil and climate. China alone produces annually nearly a million and a half tons of tea; to say nothing of the teas of Japan, Corea, Assam, and Java.

Effects of Tea.

Tea exhilarates without intoxicating; rouses the mind to increased activity without reaction, while at the same time it soothes the body, dispels headache, and counteracts the effects of fermented liquors and narcotics. It lessens also the waste of the tissues under the labors of life.

As an English authority says: "When the time has arrived to the old and infirm, that the stomach can no longer digest enough of the ordinary elements of food to keep up the waste of the system, and the size and weight of the body begins to diminish, tea comes in as a medicine to arrest this loss of tissue." No wonder then that the aged, the infirm and the poor should take kindly to tea. If supplies of food are scanty it lessens the need for them, while it makes them feel more light and cheerful, and contributes to their enjoyment.

Black and Green Teas.

Either may be prepared at will from the same leaves; the difference lies in the mode of treatment. The earliest leaves are the tenderest and best flavored; later gatherings grow more woody and bitter. Black teas are spread in the air for some time after gathering, then roasted and rolled by hand, again exposed to the air, whereby they undergo a slight degree of fermentation, and finally are dried slowly over charcoal fires. The leaves for green tea are, as soon as gathered, roasted a few minutes in pans over a brisk fire, after which they are carefully rolled and thoroughly dried.

Analysis of Tea by Dr. Hassall.

	Black.	Green.
Water	11.56	9.37
Tannin	15.24	18.69
Gum	5.70	5.89
Albuminous matter	15.55	24.39
Theine	2.53	2.79
Ash	5.82	5.38
Chlorophyle, etc	5.24	1.83
Cellulose and other matter insoluble in water	38.36	31.66
	100.00	100.00

The aroma and commercial value of tea are due to a small quantity, (from ¼ to 1 per cent.) of a volatile oil which it contains. This oil, as in coffee, is developed by roasting, the fresh picked leaves having neither an astringent, aromatic, nor bitter taste. But the effects of tea are due to its theine and tannin. Theine is present in all kinds of tea, as well as in coffee and cocoa, but it has no flavor. Tannin forms from a fifth to a seventh of the weight of the dried tea leaf, and is the more completely extracted the longer the tea is infused, or "draws." Its precise effect upon the system is not fully known. Black tea contains less theine, essential oil, and tannin, than green tea.

The Chinese pour hot water upon their tea, and drink it clear, and in Russia a squeeze of lemon takes the place of our cream. The Chinese sometimes flavor their fine teas with the cowslip colored blossoms of the sweet-scented olive and other odoriferous plants; and they also adulterate them with foreign or exhausted tea leaves, or with tea dust, called "Lie tea." But good authorities declare that fair grades of tea are not now much or necessarily adulterated, and that the old idea that green teas are colored or faced with copper is erroneous; at least experts have not been able to detect even traces of it.

Tea Made to Order.

There are tea coloring and facing establishments in this country which use for the purpose substances very similar to those used by the Chinese, and they have become so expert of late years that they can turn a black tea into a green (or vice versa) at short notice.

Tea buyers judge quality by the aroma, flavor, and the color and strength of the infusion. They detect vegetable adulterations by the shape and size of the leaf when unrolled, and sometimes burn the leaves and weigh the residue of ash.

Gunpowder, Hyson, and Imperial.

Some of the most experienced tea dealers in New York declare that there is really no essential difference in the quality of the "Firsts" or choicest grades of any "Chop" of either Gunpowder, Hyson, or Imperial, the only difference being in the form or fineness of granulation. But the popular preference in green tea is for Gunpowder, which is believed to consist of the first leaves or leaf buds of the plant. It is graded from "common" or "fair" up to "choicest."

Varieties of Tea.

Hyson is a widely used green tea. The name is derived from He-chun, a noted Chinese tea grower. Young Hyson is said to be made from the earlier leaves; Imperials and Hysons from later gatherings. Hyson skin is the light inferior leaves winnowed out. Twankay is the poorest of the green, as Bohea is of the black teas. Pekoe is the best of black teas, but is little used, except to give fragrance to mixtures. "Capers" is used similarly to flavor green teas. Congou (made with care) and Souchong are good black teas, and are the so-called "English Breakfast Teas." Moyune teas are considered as among the best and healthiest of green teas, while Pingsuys are inferior. Cheap teas are most adulterated. Fine teas are not only better in flavor, but are stronger and go further.

Oolong teas have "the call" in popularity with the Americans just now and they are recommended in sickness by the best physicians. There are three kinds, the Formosa, Foo Chow, and Amoy. The first two are the best. An article in the *London Daily News*, of February 18, 1888, avers that the Chinese are growing neglectful in cultivating, firing, and fermenting their teas, and that Japan is stealing away the green tea trade of China, as India and Ceylon are taking that in black tea.

Japan Teas.

A. & A. Low, of New York, imported the first cargo of Japan tea about twenty years ago, and since then its consumption has constantly increased. The natural leaf is yellowish brown, and the first Japan teas brought here were of that color. But the tint has changed. The "uncolored" Japan tea is in fact now all colored with some substance like the Chinese green teas, but not injuriously. The "Basket fired" is the nearest to the uncolored leaf. The "Sun-dried" is very popular here, and is but slightly colored. Expert tea tasters declare that Japan teas are more exciting to the nerves than those from China.

Blended Teas.

New crop teas are the best. Japan teas come in June, and Chinese later, say in July and August. Many prefer a mixture of green and black tea for family use, and retail dealers often have the knack of so blending the two that the excellence of each is enhanced. Such a combination has less effect upon the nerves, and is less expensive than good green tea, while it may be more delightful in flavor than either black or green tea alone.

COFFEE.

Coffee has been aptly called the "Beverage of Intelligence." It quickens the functions of the brain, arouses all the intellectual faculties, stimulates and gives clearness to thought and increases the powers of judgment. It exhilarates the nervous system, counteracts the stupor caused by fatigue, by disease, or by opium, allays hunger, retards the waste of the tissues, fortifies the powers of endurance, and to a certain extent gives to the weary and exhausted increased strength and vigor, and a feeling of comfort and repose.

Both tea and coffee are more and more used in proportion to the intellectual development of modern times. But coffee does not excite the nervous system as greatly as tea and there is less reaction after it.

Coffee Better than Alcohol.

Coffee tends to lessen the desire for alcoholic drinks, and possesses some of their properties without their bad effects. Alcohol is a false and dangerous friend. Its free use enfeebles the vital organs, reduces the power of resistance, degrades the mind and body and leads on to poverty, disease, and death. Coffee produces the beneficial effects of moderate doses of alcohol, without its injurious effects. It does not, like alcohol, destroy the nerves, or invite immoderation, and even when used to excess is incapable of doing serious injury.

The most temperate countries are those which consume most coffee, and in the light of all these facts it would appear that efforts to extend and increase the use of coffee tend to check or diminish alcoholism.

Coffee Growth and Production.

Coffee plants are raised from the seed, are set out in 12 months, 450 plants to the acre, begin to bear in 4 years, mature in 7 years, and continue for 40 years. The flowers are white and fragrant; the fruit, which grows in clusters, resembles a red cherry and contains two seeds, which are the coffee of commerce.

The world's total annual production of coffee is about 666,000 tons, of which Brazil furnishes 360,000 tons. The entire population of the United States averages to consume, per capita 7 $\frac{48}{100}$ lbs. of coffee yearly, more than three-quarters of which comes from Brazil.

RAW COFFEE, unlike tea, improves in quality with age, while it shrinks in weight, and inferior coffees may in time equal the choicest varieties. The aroma is in the direct ratio of its drying by keeping. Inferior coffees are uneven, often unclean. The large, uniform, dense, heavy grains are preferred, as showing complete maturity and careful selection. The color varies from all shades of yellow to tints of brown, green, and bluish green. There are large establishments in one or more eastern cities, which assort, color, and polish raw coffees. Much Brazilian coffee is assorted and sold for Mocha, Java, etc. Real Mocha is small, round, and dark yellow; Java and East Indian is larger and of a paler yellow. Ceylon, Brazilian and West Indian have naturally a bluish green or greenish grey tint.

ROASTING is necessary to develop the aroma and goodness

of coffee. This delicate operation changes its chemical composition and develops the caffeine and volatile oil. If roasted too little the coffee retains a raw taste; if too much, a part is changed to charcoal and much aroma lost. The outside may be burned and the inside left raw, or some grains may be half raw and others burned. Coffee loses in weight from 15 to 20 and even 25 per cent., and gains in bulk from 30 to 60 per cent., according as it is roasted to a reddish, chestnut, or dark brown. The best roasting is that which reduces the weight about sixteen per cent., or to a light chestnut brown.

Coffee and Tea Compared.

Tea yields, weight for weight, twice as much caffeine (or theine) as coffee; but as we use more in weight of the latter, a cup of coffee contains about as much caffeine as a cup of tea. The composition of roasted coffee and the tea leaf are given as follows, although the proportions are variable:

	Tea.	Coffee.
Water	8	5
Theine or caffeine......................	2½	¾
Tannin..................................	14	4
Essential oil...........................	½	Trace.
Minor extractives......................	15	36
Insoluble organic matter................	54½	50
Ash....................................	5½	4¼
	100	100

Modes of Making Coffee.

One pound of the properly roasted bean or berry should make 55 or 60 cups of good coffee. Coffee may be made too bitter, but it is impossible to make it too fragrant. Coffee is much the best when freshly ground. The French and many Americans merely steep or infuse their coffee at a temperature just below the boiling point, claiming that boiling dissipates the aroma; others bring it only to a boil; while others still, hold that boiling it a little is more economical, as giving an increased quantity of the soluble, exhilarating and bitter principles. Soft water is best for coffee, and coffee is better cold than warmed over, as it then loses its fragrance.

Coffee Substitutes and Adulterations.

Rye, beans, peas, acorns, carrots, turnips, dandelion root, burned bread, and many similar substances have at times been used as substitutes or adulterants for coffee. But as none of them contain caffeine or the volatile aromatic oil, they cannot serve the same physiological principle. Ground coffee is extensively adulterated, and mainly with the much cheaper

Chicory or Wild Endive.

Roasting develops in this root an empyreumatic, volatile oil which exercises upon the system some of the nerve-soothing, hunger-staying effects of tea and coffee. A little chicory gives as dark a color and as bitter a taste as a great deal of coffee. It is not unwholesome unless taken in excess, when its effects are bad. It is a poor substitute for coffee, but some peeple seem actually to prefer coffee which contains chicory.

Tests for Adulterations.

If ground coffee cakes in the paper, or when pinched by the fingers, or if, when a little is put into water, a part sinks while the rest swims, and the water becomes immediately discolored, the coffee is probably adulterated. The more caking and discoloration, the more chicory and the less value.

There are numerous brands of ground coffee on the market, and some of them are very popular and satisfactory. There are also various kinds of "Extracts" and "Essences" of coffee, and even humble chicory may sometimes be seen without disguise and nicely put up in yellow papers.

Cocoa and Chocolate.

The theobroma tree grows in Central and South America. The seeds of its fruit, which are about the size of almonds, are gently roasted, deprived of their husks and ground to a paste. This is Cocoa. If this paste be mixed with sugar and flavored with vanilla, bitter almonds, etc., it forms the well known, delicious, and nourishing Chocolate, which may either be eaten as a confection or drank as a beverage. The husk, which forms about 10 per cent. of the weight of the bean, is called "Shells," and used by invalids and others for making a light and delicate infusion or tea.

The aroma of cocoa is due to an essential oil which is developed, as with tea and coffee, by roasting. Its exhilarating principle, theobromine, resembles theine. It contains a large percentage of fat, is very rich and nutritious, and may be said to unite in itself the inspiring properties of tea with the strength-giving qualities of milk.

Starch, as well as sugar, is sometimes added to cocoa and chocolate by the manufacturers, and the practice is believed to be justified, owing to their richness in oil and as better fitting them for digestion. Cocoa is, however, also prepared free from starch and deprived of a portion of its oil. There are many preparations of chocolate and cocoa in market, and they embrace all grades of purity, sweetness and price.

DAIRY PRODUCTS.

Milk, Etc.

Milk is sophisticated by robbing it of its cream, or by adding to it "The milk of the cow with the iron tail," and by coloring it. CREAM contains about 40 per cent. of fat and 55 per cent. of water ; SKIMMED MILK is water, with sugar and caseine. WHEY is merely a solution of milk sugar with a little albumen. Milk is best and most plentiful in spring, and richer but less abundant in dry seasons. The last milk drawn from the cow contains most cream. KOUMISS, the use of which is rapidly increasing, is well skimmed milk, treated with a lactic ferment for 30 or 40 hours. It is very easy of digestion. CONDENSED MILK is ordinary milk evaporated so that three pints are reduced to one. It soon spoils unless the air is excluded. PRESERVED MILK in cans contains about one-third its weight of sugar.

Butter.

Good, fresh butter, contains 84 to 88 parts of milk fat, 10 or 12 parts of moisture, and a little milk sugar, caseine and salt. Inferior butter may contain as much as 33 per cent. of water, or buttermilk, and salt. The more buttermilk left in, the sooner the butter grows rancid, while over-working tends to make it soft and oily. The melting of butter changes its physical properties, and long exposure to the air injures the best butter.

Good butter is solid and of a grained texture, has a fine orange yellow color and a pleasant aroma. It may comfort the curious to know that its odor is due to a very little butyric acid, combined with oxide of lipyle. To test the quantity of moisture, put a little of the butter in a bottle, heat gently, and leave near the fire for half an hour, when the butter will rise, leaving the water and salt at the bottom. Two-thirds of all the butter made is colored.

Classification of Butter.

The New York Mercantile Exchange classification, which is standard, is as follows: EASTERN CREAMERY, SWEET CREAM CREAMERY, DAIRY BUTTER; WESTERN CREAMERY, IMITATION CREAMERY, and DAIRY, also "LADLE" and "GREASE BUTTER."

CREAMERY BUTTER is the best. It is such as is made from the cream obtained by setting the milk at the creamery, or by the system known as "Cream gathering," by which the farmer delivers his cream to the creamery to be churned or made into butter. Butter made under the former system, or from the milk, is better than that made from the gathered cream. SWEET CREAM CREAMERY is made from unfermented cream.

DAIRY BUTTER is that which is made, salted, and packed by the dairyman or farmer. Though often really excellent, it is less uniform in quality, and therefore less reliable.

LADLE BUTTER.—This is butter of all seasons, ages, and qualities, collected by the dealer, in rolls, lumps, or packages, from the farm houses, salted, or unsalted, as the case may be, and by him reworked, resalted, colored, and packed.

GRADES OF BUTTER.—The varieties are all graded again into "Extras," "Extra Firsts," "Firsts," "Seconds," "Thirds," etc. "EXTRAS" are the choicest grades under each classification, and must come up to the following standard. Flavor must be perfect if fresh made, and fine if held; body perfect and uniform, color good for the season when made, perfect and uniform; must be properly salted, and in good and uniform packages. "Extra Firsts' must be a grade just below "Extras," and fine butter; good color, etc., etc. "Firsts" must be clean and sweet, sound and good. "Seconds" must be fair throughout, may be strong if held, on tops and sides of package. "Thirds" may be off-flavored, etc. "Poor Butter" may be strong, and of all grades below "Thirds" down to "Grease Butter."

Artificial Butter.

About 20 years ago a French chemist tried to imitate the process which takes place when cows are underfed, and when, therefore, the butter they yield is supplied from their own fat. His aim was to make a substitute for butter for the poor, etc., which should be healthful, agreeable and cheap, and which should keep a long time without becoming rancid. The man's name was Mege-Mouries, and he discovered Oleomargarine. This product has been, and is still extensively manufactured in the United States, and is pronounced by some of the most eminent and scientific men to be wholesome, nutritious and palatable.

Oleomargarine is made from the fat of slaughtered cattle. This is melted at a temperature of 150 deg. F., and the stearine extracted. The "Oleo oil" which is left is now churned with cream or milk, colored and salted.

Butterine is made from oleo oil, neutral lard, and some butter. These ingredients are churned with milk or cream, colored, salted and packed in tubs. Refined cotton seed oil is also frequently used in the manufacture of both products.

Oleomargarine Laws.

In 1886 Congress passed the "Oleomargarine Bill," defining butter to be an article made solely from milk and cream. It imposes a tax of two cents per pound upon oleomargarine and similar butter substitutes, compels their sale in certain sized packages, plainly marked or branded with the name of their contents, and requires manufacturers and dealers to take out special licenses, all under heavy penalties. Some of the State laws, restricting the sale of oleomargarine, are still more stringent, and its consumption has diminished, although it is still used in some sections and extensively exported.

Cheese.

No article of food appears to be more affected than cheese by slight variations of the materials from which it is made, or by such apparently trifling differences in the methods of manufacture. Both full and skimmed milk are used; the former yielding, of course, the best product. The latter cheese is little used in this country. An English writer says that if milk is skimmed for several days, "it yields a cheese so hard that pigs grunt at it, dogs bark at it, but neither dare bite it." People's tastes vary greatly in the flavor of cheese, and while some prefer the natural tint, others buy that which is colored. Color adds neither richness nor flavor, and is gradually falling into disuse.

Cheese as a Staple Food.

Some nations (as Great Britain, etc.,) consume cheese largely as a staple food, while others use it more sparingly, and mainly as a condiment or relish. Bread and cheese consort better with ale than with whiskey and this country is not greatly given to cheese as a staple food, although its consumption is increasing here, owing to recent improvements in the modes of manufacture and in its quality. Two-thirds of our total product now goes to Europe.

Analysis of Full and Skim Milk Cheese.

The composition of cheese is given as follows:

	Rich cheese.	Skim milk cheese.
Water...	36	44
Casein	29	45
Milk fat	30½	6
Salt and phosphates	4½	5

Good and Poor Cheese.

Cheese dries fast and shrinks in weight; hence the grocer who sells it in small quantities is compelled to charge a fair margin or advance upon its cost to save himself from loss. The ordinary weight of American cheeses is about 60 lbs., but smaller

ones are growing in favor, and many are now made weighing from
35 to 40 lbs.   A grocer who has a good class of custom soon
realizes that our poor cheese takes the place of several good ones,
and it is his aim to secure a good and popular quality and
stick to it.

Facts About Cheese.

The best cheese is made from the rich June grasses, the poorest
in the heats of summer.   June cheese is safest to keep, as the
curds are then scalded higher, to ensure that they will sustain the
coming warm weather.   Cheese may be made for immediate use
—and such will grow sharp if long kept—or it may be so made
as to keep a year or more with constant improvement or ripening.
It requires about ten pounds of milk to make one pound of
cheese.

"FILLED" CHEESE is made by substituting lard in place of the
cream of the milk.   Ten pounds of such cheese contains about 1
pound of lard.   This product is largely made in some sections,
and is chiefly sold in the South or exported.

Classification of Cheese.

Cheese made in New York, Pennsylvania and Wisconsin has
the first "Call" in the New York Mercantile Exchange.
"FANCY" must be full cream, perfect in flavor, close made, well
cured, of uniform color and perfect surface.   "FINE" is the next
grade below—must be also full cream, clean flavor, etc. "KNOWN
MARKS" or FACTORY CHEESE may not be full cream.   "WESTERN
CHEESE" "Shall include those of all States not mentioned above
and shall be classified as fancy, fine, and known marks, but they
may not be full cream."

Imported Cheese.

SWISS CHEESE comes from Switzerland, and more of this is imported than of all others combined.   Next stands EDAM from Holland.   The delicious ROQUEFORT CHEESE, made in France, from
ewes milk and kept in mountain caves to ripen, stands third in
the list of imported cheeses, and PARMESAN stands fourth; it is
made from skimmed milk, the curd hardened by a gentle heat.

This and SBRINZ cheese are used for soups—grated. GORGONZOLA is a fine, rich, Italian cheese, each weighing about ten pounds. Other good Italian cheeses are made from the milk of the buffalo which feed on the Roman Campagna. STILTON is the finest of English cheeses. It is made from full milk with added cream. It .improves with age, and is best when at least two years old. The CHEDDAR, CHESHIRE and QUEEN's ARMS are other varieties of good English cheese.

Eggs.

Eggs are cheap and substantial food. The white is mostly albumen, while the yolk is two-thirds oil. Turkeys eggs are pronounced the best in flavor. Guinea hens eggs are excellent, and keep well on account of their thick shells. Goose eggs are larger, whiter, and less esteemed. Duck eggs are bluish, and less desirable than hens eggs. Eight hens eggs weigh a pound.

A fresh egg feels heavy in the hand and is semi transparent before the light. Its large end feels warm to the tongue. The older it is, the less pleasant and nutritious it becomes. If it stands upright in water it is bad; if obliquely it is not quite fresh. If it lies at the bottom it is quite fresh. An egg begins to lose flavor a few hours after it has been laid.

Lard.

Good, pure lard should be white, should melt without ebullition or sputtering, be almost as clear and white as water, and not deposit any sediment. It is composed of oleine 62 parts, stearine 65 parts. The fat of the hog taken from around the kidneys and the layers over the ribs is called "Leaf lard" and is better, firmer and will stand warm weather better, than lard made from the entire fat of the animal.

LARD ADMIXTURES.—There is no complaint that lard is adulterated with substances injurious to health; but in February, 1888, a leading lard manufacturer testified before the Senate Committee on Agriculture, at Washington, that seven-eighths of the lard now on the market is made from the entire fat of the hog, refined and purified, and mixed with a proportion of refined cotton seed oil and about 15 per cent. of stearine, to give it hardness. This, he claimed, is preferred by the public generally to strictly pure lard. The testimony of Prof. Sharpless, of Boston, given at the same time and place, substantially bore out this statement as to the ingredients used, although in the many analyses of American lard made by him, he found some brands which were absolutely pure hog products. Lard is sometimes adulterated with water, but this may be easily detected by melting it, evaporating the water, and reweighing.

Lard may be had in barrels, wooden and tin tubs and pails, and in one pound tin cups. It is also retailed in bulk, like butter.

Fresh Meats and Poultry.

BEEF.—Good beef should be juicy, somewhat firm and elastic, velvety and smooth grained to the touch, and "marbled" with little streaks, dots or points of fat. The suet fat should be plentiful, white, firm, dry, and crumbly; if the fat is yellow, oily, or fibrous, the beef is inferior.

MUTTON is wholesome, nutritious, and easily digested. The best is from a plump, small boned animal, with abundant white, clear, solid fat. The lean should be firm, dark red, and juicy, the leg bones clear, white, and short. GOOD LAMB has hard, white fat and reddish bones.

PORK is best in fall and winter. The skin should be thin and pearly, the lean a delicate red, juicy, firm, and finely grained, and the fat white. If the fat is yellow and soft, the pork is inferior. Pork is dangerous if not thoroughly cooked.

VEAL should be from a good sized, reasonably fat milk or stall fed calf, five to ten weeks old. The fat should be firm and white, but not too white; the meat finely grained, fairly firm, and juicy.

POULTRY.—Many farmers have found that it pays better to feed their grain to poultry than to sell it by the bushel, and poultry is therefore much more abundant, cheaper, and more

widely consumed than ever before. The dry-picked or unscalded
has the preference in price. The best have short legs and small
bones, and are plump. If fresh, the eyes are bright and full, the
feet and legs moist and limber. If stale, poultry looks dark and
slimy. When chickens grow to be a year old they are called fowl;
the legs grow rougher, the skin fat and tougher, and the rear
end of the breast bone hard. A moderate sized TURKEY is more
apt to be tender than a very large one.

Smoked and Dried Meats and Fish.

HAMS, ETC.—The best are of medium size, weighing, say,
from 8 to 14 pounds, plump, round, and the bone small. The
shank should be short and tapering, skin thin and not shriveled
or wrinkled, and the fat white and firm. To ascertain if ham
has begun to spoil, thrust a skewer or knife in at the side of the
aitch bone and at the knuckle joint; if sound there, it is good
throughout. BACON.—This is the smoked flank. BREAKFAST
BACON, made from young pigs, is very delicate and palatable.
BEEF TONGUES are a delicacy, whether fresh, smoked, or pickled,
hot or cold. The best are thick, firm, and with plenty of fat on
the under side of the base.

DRIED COD.—This is an important grocers' staple. The largest and best are caught on the "Banks" or in the deep waters
off the Eastern coast. Some are sold whole and others are deprived
of the back bone. Codfish is also prepared for market by being
boned, skinned, trimmed, and even shredded. Other and inferior fish, such as Haddock, Hake, Pollock, etc., are often sold for
cod, when salted, and especially when prepared as above.

HERRING, smoked whole, or scaled and boneless, are
widely consumed. The freshest, fattest, and largest are best.
Smoked SALMON, HALIBUT, and STURGEON, are appetizing relishes
for the summer tea table. There are also EELS pickled in jelly.
SARDELLES—small fish packed in highly salted milk, smoked
SPRATS, ANCHOVIES, etc.

Salt or Pickled Fish.

Mackerel have the front rank in this line, and there are few

good tables on which they do not occasionally appear. They are
sold by the grocer in barrels and fractions of barrels, in kits of
20, 15, and 10 pounds, in tins, minus heads and tails, and by the
single fish. The best are the fattest, largest, and freshest of the
current season. They should be free from rust and soaked before cooking until all the brine is drawn out. They can be
afterwards salted, if necessary. They are graded as "Extra" and
"Fancy" "Shores" and "Bays," and vary in size and fatness,
as numbers 1, 2, 3 and 4.

SALMON, ETC.—Both Halifax and Oregon salmon are pickled
or salted, and in demand in many sections of the country, and
pickled SALMON BELLIES are very fine. HERRING and COD are
also to be had in brine.

Meat Essences and Extracts.

There are several varieties of these articles in liquids, pastes,
and solids. Some, at least, of them, without being true nutrients
are excellent as condiments, stimulants, and tonics for digestion.
Meat juices contain a substance called kreatine, which is similar
in its exhilerating properties to the peculiar principles of tea and
coffee. Fifty pounds of meat are said to be required to make one
pound of Liebig's meat extract. These preparations are valuable
additions to other foods, but all that is needed for nourishment
should be added to them.

CANNED GOODS.

Until lately, man had done little more in preserving his food
in a fresh condition, than the squirrels which gather and store
their nuts and seeds in a warm, dry place. To be sure, he knew
how to dry and smoke, and the uses of salt and sugar. He had
even tried to preserve his meats and fruits in a fresh state; but
his rude methods hardly foreshadowed the splendid results which
have recently been achieved in the line of canned goods.

Excellence of American Canned Goods.

M. Appert, of France, first patented (in 1810) a process for preserving animal and vegetable substances in close vessels of glass—after subjecting them to the action of heat—and an English firm soon after introduced provisions preserved in tin. But it was reserved for Americans to lead the world, not only in the magnitude of their canning industries, but also in the art of preserving meats, vegetables, and fruits, by processes so delicate and effective, as to retain their original shape and texture, as well as their freshness and flavor. And, moreover, while they have practically prolonged the "Seasons" for perishable food products throughout the entire year, and furnish them for the consumer at very reasonable rates, the producer has often thanked them for giving stability to prices in seasons of great "Gluts" and abundance.

Varieties of Canned Goods.

Among canned goods, in glass or tin packages of various sizes, qualities and prices, are the following:

Canned Meats.

CORNED BEEF, boiled; ROAST. BEEF, BEEF A LA MODE, BOILED HAM, BOILED TONGUE, ROAST MUTTON, ROAST VEAL, ROAST CHICKEN, ROAST TURKEY, BRAWN, POTTED MEATS of all kinds; GAME PATES of WILD DUCK, GROUSE, PARTRIDGE, PLOVER, WOODCOCK; BONED TURKEY AND CHICKEN, with jelly; CURRIED CHICKEN, DEVILLED CHICKEN, TURKEY, HAM, PIG'S FEET, LAMB'S TONGUES, etc.

Canned Soups and Broths.

BEEF, CHICKEN, GREEN TURTLE, OXTAIL, JULIENNE, MOCK TURTLE, CONSOMME, MACCARONI, VERMICELLI, PEA, MUTTON BROTH, etc.

Fish.

CLAMS, CLAM CHOWDER, ANCHOVIES, CRABS FRESH, CRABS DEVILLED, CODFISH BALLS, MACKEREL FRESH, LOBSTER, OYSTERS, PRAWNS, SHRIMP, SALMON, SARDINES, TROUT, TURTLE, KIPPERED HERRING, BLOATERS, etc.

Canned Vegetables.

ASPARAGUS, Baked, Lima, and String BEANS, GREEN CORN, MUSHROOMS, OKRA, ONIONS, PEAS, PUMPKIN, SQUASH, SUCCOTASH, SPINACH, RHUBARB, etc.

Canned Fruits.

APPLES, APRICOTS, BLACKBERRIES, BLUEBERRIES, CHERRIES, GRAPES, GOOSEBERRIES, PEACHES, PEARS, PLUMS, PINEAPPLES, QUINCES, RASPBERRIES, STRAWBERRIES, etc.

Canned Sundries.

Besides the above, there are "Heaps" of canned delicacies, such, for instance, as TRUFFLES, TRUFFLE PATES, TRUFFLE DU PERIGORD, in tins and glass, PLUM PUDDINGS, PLUM PUDDING SAUCES, etc.

Some of the French vegetables in glass and tin are beautifully green in appearance, but it is evident that they are artificially colored. A more wholesome device is to put the articles up in the intensely green bottles sometimes seen.

THE TIN CANS.—Tin is mainly used for canned goods, and is the least objectionable of all the metals, and better than anything probably, except glass. It does not oxidize easily, and if it does, its soluble salts are less injurious. than those of any other available metal.

Jellies, Preserves, etc.

Jellies are made from nearly all the fruits by mixing their juices with sugar, and often with gelatine or isinglass, (four parts of which will convert 100 parts of water into a tremulous jelly) and boiling them down. Jellies are wholesome, cooling, and grateful, provided they are free from adulterations and noxious colorings, and are much used upon the tea table and in the sick room. Among the varieties of jelly in the market are APPLE, CRAB APPLE, BLACKBERRY, CURRANT, GRAPE, LEMON, GUAVA, ORANGE, QUINCE, RASPBERRY, STRAWBERRY, etc. They come in tumblers and jars, and in bulk. There are also CALVES' FOOT, WINE and SPIRIT jellies.

PRESERVES.—All the above fruits are preserved in sugar, and put up in quart and pint jars. CHERRIES, PEACHES, PEARS, etc., are also preserved in BRANDY, and sold in glass jars. There is also a great variety of JAMS and MARMALADES, both foreign and domestic; GINGER ROOT, boiled in syrup, etc. FRUIT BUTTER is made from various fruits, as, Apple, Cranberry, Peach, Pear, or Raspberry, etc., by stewing them in sugar or molasses. It is usually sold from pails by the pound, and is much used in some sections.

Flavoring Extracts and Essences.

The delicate flavors of fruit and the fragrant principles of spice and other substances, as vanilla, etc., are extracted by pressure or distillation, and dissolved in spirits of wine for culinary purposes. It is found also, that certain ethers and oils may be so combined (as, for instance, potato oil) as to yield the taste and smell of many fruits, such as pears, apples, grapes pineapples, etc. Flavoring extracts and essences are variously put up in vials and bottles; among them are LEMON, VANILLA, ROSE, ALMOND, PEACH, CELERY, GINGER, CLOVES, NUTMEG, STRAWBERRY, RASPBERRY, PINEAPPLE, NECTARINE, etc.

ISINGLASS AND GELATINE are used to make jellies, and thicken soups and gravies. Isinglass is made from the intestines of fish. Its advantages over gelatine are lighter color, less flavor, and greater thickening power. In cold water it softens, swells, becomes white and opaque. In hot water it smells a little fishy. Gelatine is made from the bones of animals; it also swells in cold water, but becomes glassy and transparent, while in hot water it has somewhat the smell of glue. It is often sold for isinglass. The test of both is in the fineness and clearness of their jelly. CALVES' FOOT JELLY is delicate, but less firm. Gelatine is sold in sheets and shreds.

HERBS for seasoning, as, SAGE, SUMMER SAVORY, SWEET MAR-JORAM, THYME, etc., are sold in the leaf, and also powdered, in tins and paper packets.

Spices and Condiments.

Spices are generally understood to be more aromatic and fragrant and less pungent than what are called condiments. Spices are usually added to sweetened food, while condiments, as pepper and mustard, are better suited to meats and food containing salt.

It is impossible to supply genuine articles if the public are not willing to pay for them, and it may be accepted as a general rule, that the lower the price of ground spices and condiments, the more they are adulterated. The materials chiefly used for this purpose are starch, cracker dust and similar harmless substances, and the mixture usually contains as much of the pure material as can reasonably be afforded at the price it sells for. The purchaser may elect whether he will have such articles, or those which are genuine at a higher cost. The grocer does not create wants and demands; he merely supplies them.

PEPPER.—There are two kinds, black and white. Both are from the seeds of the *piper nigrum*, a plant which grows in the East and West Indies. BLACK PEPPER is the seed picked before it is fully ripe, dried and ground. WHITE PEPPER is made from the ripened seed deprived of its black outer shell or pericarp. Pepper is an agreeable addition to many kinds of food, and is said to promote the secretion of the gastric juice; it is more used than any other spice.

CAYENNE PEPPER is the powdered pod of one or more species of capsicum. The sharp taste is due to a camphor like substance found more in the pods than in the seeds.

MUSTARD.—This is the flour of the black or white mustard seed. The black seed contains most volatile oil, is more pungent, and differs from the white in chemical composition. The two are blended in various proportions. Wheat flour is often added, with a little turmeric to bring up the color. Mustard seed contains over 30 per cent. of a fixed oil, and a portion of this is often extracted. This practice is considered beneficial rather than fraudulent.

GINGER.—This is the root-stalk of a plant which grows in Jamaica and other warm countries. The best comes with the skin scraped off. This is ground. The odor of ginger is due to an essential oil; its pungency to a peculiar resin. It is sometimes adulterated with starch, sago, rice, and wheat flour, mustard hulls, cayenne pepper, etc. But, as with all the other spices, there are pure brands.

CLOVES are the dried flower buds of the clove tree. They come from the East Indies, Africa, and South America, ranking in value in the order named. The best contain as much as 16 per cent. of a volatile oil to which their flavor is due. Ground cloves have sometimes a portion of this oil pressed out, with piminto or allspice added, which latter is much less costly. Cloves are best when large, plump, bright in tint, and full of oil, which exudes on pressure with the finger nail.

ALLSPICE OR PIMENTO is the little, round berry of an evergreen tree, common in the West Indies. It contains about 4 per cent. of an aromatic oil. Owing to its cheapness, it is less adulterated than other spices.

CINNAMON is the true bark of a small evergreen tree of Ceylon. The best is very thin, the outer and inner coats of the bark having been removed.

CASSIA is the bark of another species of cinnamon tree; it is thicker, corky, and not so red. It is cheap and not much adulterated. It is often sold for cinnamon, but is less aromatic and valuable. CASSIA BUDS are the unripe buds of the same tree.

NUTMEGS AND MACE.—Nutmegs are the seeds of the *Myristica. Fragrans*, a tree which grows in the East Indies. Good nutmegs feel heavy in the hand, and are not worm eaten. They contain about 8 per cent. of volatile oil, and 25 per cent. of fixed oil, which exudes under indentation or pressure with the finger nail. Most people buy whole nutmegs and the ground article has only a limited sale. MACE is the arillus or coating of the nutmeg, and is also sold whole or unground

CURRY POWDER.—This compound of spices, etc., is much used in India and other hot countries, as an appetizer and stimulant to digestion. There are several excellent brands of curry powder in market, both English and American, made approximately after some one of the following five receipts:

	Proportions.				
Turmeric	6	4	6	3	2
Black pepper	5	4	2	2	½
Cayenne	1	1	0	¼	6
Ginger	0	2	3	0	½
Fenugreek	3	2	0	1	¼
Cummin seed	3	2	2	4	0
Coriander seed	0	6	8	12	6
Cardamom seed	0	0	½	½	0
Pimento	0	0	½	¼	¼
Cinnamon	0	0	0	¼	¼
Cloves	0	0	0	¼	1
Nutmeg	0	0	0	0	½

Salt.

COMMON SALT varies in purity and sometimes contains salts of lime, magnesia, and potash. But as those are more soluble in water than common salt, it is easy to remove them in the process of manufacture. Our culinary salt comes from several sources; rock salt deposits or mines, sea water, and salt springs.

There are numerous brands of salt which are freed from all impurity, ground to various degrees of fineness, and put up in barrels, sacks, bags and packets of all sizes; also in stone jars.

CELERY SALT is good common salt mingled with the finely ground seeds of celery.

Besides the finer qualities for table use, there are varieties specially adapted for salting and pickling meats, fish, etc.; lump rock salt for cattle, hay salt, etc. The bitter salts of lime, magnesia, etc., attract moisture more than common salt. hence dryness is a sign of purity.

Vinegar.

The sour principle is acetic acid, of which good vinegar contains about four per cent. Vinegar may be obtained by fermentation from the juice of any starchy or sweet fruit or vegetable, from beet, or even from sweetened water, to which "mother" or other vinegar is added. Cider vinegar is most used, as it retains the fruity flavor of the apple, but good vinegar is also made from wine, malt, oranges, raspberries, etc. There are many varieties

In market, both domestic and foreign. Stringent laws regulate the purity and strength of vinegar for domestic uses, in New York and some other states.

Pickles.

These are fruits and vegetables preserved in vinegar, after first steeping them in brine. Certain articles require to be pickled in scalding hot vinegar, others with cold; salt, pepper and spices are added to suit the taste. Pickles were formerly extensively colored green with copper, but the ghastly practice has gone out of date. Intelligent people will prefer those which have the more natural and wholesome yellowish, olive green tint. There are all sorts of pickles in market, put up in glass or wood packages of various sizes, as follows:

CUCUMBERS and GHERKINS, CHOW CHOW, CAULIFLOWER, ONIONS, MANGOES, PICALILLI, WALNUTS, PEPPERS, HORSERADISH, MIXED PICKLES, and SWEET PICKLES. Among the best of imported pickles are the reliable Cross and Blackwell goods; some domestic brands are perhaps equally good. OLIVES are in brine, usually in wide-mouthed glass jars. They come from Italy, Spain, and France. The "Queen," "Crescent," etc., are favorite brands. There are also French CAPERS, so important as an accompaniment for boiled mutton, etc.

SALAD OIL.—The best is the oil of the OLIVE, which, when pure, is of pale, greenish yellow tint, with an agreeable odor and taste. Refined COTTONSEED OIL has naturally a more reddish tint. It is extensively sold as olive oil or mixed with it, although many grocers keep the genuine olive oil. SALAD DRESSINGS are also in market, some of which are very fine and delicate.

Sauces.

These articles give zest to food and stimulate digestion. Their composition is very varied and embraces many fruits and vegetables, as the tomato, walnut, garlic, shallot; many herbs, as tarragon, chervill, mint, thyme, marjoram; many condiments, as cayenne, black pepper, mustard, and all the spices; many fish, as lobsters, oysters, clams, shrimp, anchovies; the juices of meat, besides salt, sugar, molasses, etc.

PEPPER SAUCE is made from the little Jamaica peppers, the Mexican, Chili pepper, or some other variety of red or green pepper. There are numerous brands, and nearly all are good. The TABASCO PEPPER SAUCE is excellent. TOMATO CATSUP OR KETCHUP is a very wholesome and agreeable addition to the diet. Among the best and most popular varieties is the "SHREWSBURY" TOMATO KETCHUP. Mushroom and Walnut Catsups are less used, but still have many friends.

Among the dainty and well known SAUCES, are the WORCESTERSHIRE, LEICESTERSHIRE, GLOUCESTERSHIRE, SULTANA, PICCADILLY, CHUTNEE, SOHO, HARVEY, NORTH OF ENGLAND, etc. There are also various American sauces, some of which are imitations of the above or very similar in composition and flavor. Some of the English sauces are put up in elegant and artistic vases.

DOMESTIC FRUITS AND BERRIES.

The increasing excellence, abundance and cheapness of fruits and berries is full of promise for the health and vigor of the American people. They are wholesome, cooling and nutritious.

APPLES.—This noble fruit is in market the year round; new Southern apples are first marketed in April. APRICOTS are a fine small fruit which ripens in July. CHERRIES reach us from the South in May. NECTARINES come in August. PEACHES are at the height of their season in August and September. Early in the latter month they should be secured for preserving. PEARS.—The choicest are the Dutchess, Bartlett and Virgalieu. CALIFORNIA PEARS are excellent and widely sold through the country. PLUMS ripen in August, and are in season until October. QUINCE is a highly flavored fruit, used only for preserves. GRAPES.— Besides our own abundant and delicious Muscat, Concord, Isabella, Catawba, and other varieties, three-quarters of a million barrels of the hardy and cooling white Almeria grapes are annually imported at New York. They were formerly a costly luxury, but are now abundant and cheap, and will keep through the winter.

STRAWBERRIES.—The season opens with shipments from Florida early in March, and closes six months later with the product of the far North. RASPBERRIES come in June and continue until August. BLACKBERRIES ripen early in July, and are very healthful. CURRANTS ripen in July and continue until September; they are white, red and black, and are wholesome and cooling. GOOSEBERRIES may be had red, yellow, green and white. They are much used unripe, for cooking purposes. CRANBERRIES begin to reach market from Cape Cod, New Jersey, etc., about September first. The largest and darkest are the best. They are healthful and an almost indispensable adjunct to roast turkey, etc.; are also used for sauces, tarts, and pies.

Tropical Fruits.

The increased knowledge in regard to the excellence and healthfulness of these fruits has, within a few years, greatly enlarged the demand for them, and they are now sold at moderate prices in almost every city and town in the land.

ORANGES.—Those from Florida and California are richer and of finer flavor, while the Mediterranean variety are thin skinned, juicy, hardy, and will keep longer. That region sends us annually a million boxes of oranges, and the annual product of Florida and California is two million boxes. Havana oranges are not as good as they used to be, but twenty thousand barrels come to New York yearly from Cuba.

LEMONS.—A million and a half boxes of lemons are consumed yearly in this country, most of which come from Sicily, but lemon culture is increasing in Florida. Lemons vary much more in price than oranges, as a heated term or unusual sickness increases the consumption.

BANANAS AND OTHER FRUITS.—There are two varieties, the red from Cuba, and the yellow from Jamaica and the Spanish Main. The latter are the better. Bananas are in market all the year, but the season is from March to August. PINEAPPLES are exquisitely flavored fruit, much used sliced for the tea table. The season is from May to August. COCOANUTS are used grated, for making pies and puddings; they are delicious, but rather indigestible. DESSICATED COCOANUT is the meat of cocoanuts ground and dried, and mixed with powdered sugar; sometimes, also, rice, flour, or corn starch is added. It comes in packets, cans, etc.

FRESH VEGETABLES.

In the Spring and Summer months the appetite craves fresh vegetables ; and their free use, especially in those seasons, will be found excellent for the general health of the family. Spinach, for instance, is said to be beneficial in kidney complaints ; Dandelion greens are good for biliousness ; Tomatoes act upon the liver ; Celery upon the nerves ; Onion soup restores a debilitated stomach, etc., etc. In fact, it would be easy thus to go through the whole vegetable list and find each one possessing some special mission of healthfulness.

Where Early Vegetables Come From.

The Bermudas send annually about $400,000 worth of potatoes, onions, beets and tomatoes to New York, during the months of March, April and May. Florida garden produce finds its way North very early in the Spring, and later, in regular order, Georgia, South and North Carolina, and Virginia, wheel into line with their numerous productions, until, finally, our home gardeners have their season. During all this time our vegetables on sale are improving in freshness as they are drawn from sources nearer home, and prices are falling.

The Varieties.

POTATOES.—The heavier ones are more mealy and nutritious than those which are waxy and soft. There are many favorite varieties. Some are early but less mealy, others prolific but lacking in flavor, etc.—hence prices vary. SWEET POTATOES.—There are two varieties—the red and yellow—with but little difference in price. CABBAGE.—A standard vegetable the year round; the heaviest are the best. CAULIFLOWER, best from April to December; the large, creamy white, solid heads are preferred; dark or soft spots indicate staleness. ONIONS are very nutritious; their powerful odor is due to a strong smelling, volatile, sulphurized oil. There are the white or silver skinned, yellow and red. Spanish Onions are milder, and much eaten raw. GARLIC, a pungent species of the onion tribe, and very healthful; used for flavoring. LEEKS and CHIVES are allies of the onion. Leeks have large leaves, a thick stalk and small root ; Chives, used as salads, have small, spine-like leaves. CARROTS, TURNIPS, BEETS and PARSNIPS are standard vegetables to be had throughout the year; frost improves the latter.

ASPARAGUS.—A choice and health giving vegetable. Season begins in March, and it grows fibrous in July. CELERY is improved by frost, and is in its prime and cheapest during the winter months, after which it becomes tougher and stringy. CUCUMBERS. — A pleasant, cooling vegetable, but difficult of digestion, and containing little nourishment. TOMATOES are excellent food for people with weak stomachs or liver difficulties; is a vegetable that could ill be spared. Millions of bushels are canned every year, and if properly put up are nearly as good as the fresh article. PEAS.—The smaller varieties are best, should be purchased in the pods, which should be cool, crisp and green. A black spot on the pea indicates that it is too old to be at its best. BEANS, shelled and string.—The former embrace the Lima sorts. The Neapolitan or snap is considered best of the String beans. GREEN CORN comes from the South in May, and the home supply lasts till October. Ears should be well filled and milky, and not too old. Green sweet corn is the best.

RHUBARB.—Much used for sauce and pies. The leaves are said to contain oxalic acid, and must not be eaten. RADISH, said to be difficult of digestion itself, but helps to digest other food. There are two varieties, the small bulbous, or round, and the long. ARTICHOKE, a tuber like the potatoe; is pickled, used as a salad and as a vegetable. SQUASH.—The summer squash is in market from April to September. Winter squash is more substantial but less delicate. OYSTER PLANT has a grassy top, and a long, tapering, white root like a carrot; its flavor suggests that of oysters. EGG PLANT, called GUINEA SQUASH at the South, should be firm, hard, and rather under ripe, it also tastes somewhat like an oyster; the large, purple, oval shaped, is the better variety. OKRA or GUMBO.—The green seed pods are much esteemed for soups and stews, especially in the South, and are growing in favor at the North. The long green variety is considered best. LETTUCE, SPINACH, BRUSSELS SPROUTS, KALE, BEET-TOPS, DANDELION LEAVES, ETC., are used as salads and for greens.

MELONS.—MUSK-MELON, the stronger the musk odor, the finer it is; but if it appears quite ripe all over, it is over ripe and decomposing. If it has no odor, it is only fit for cattle. WATERMELON, if pressed near its center, should yield a little, and the indentation disappear when the finger is removed. If no indent can be made, the melon is too green, if the depression remains, the melon is over ripe.

BEANS, PEAS, and LENTILS.—These leguminous seeds are very nutritious and palatable, and rank high among strength-giving foods. They contain vegetable casein in place of gluten, and hence are not suitable for making bread; all these articles are more digestible if eaten with fat, and the American staple dish of Pork and Beans is really the marriage of two articles which agree very well with each other. Dried PEAS, split, or ground into meal, are much used for soups. LENTILS, which are round seeds like flattened peas, are excellent used as a vegetable, but are comparatively little known. The most popular varieties of the white beans are the Marrow, Kidney and Pea beans. There are also *Frijoles* or black beans, Lima beans, etc.

DRIED FRUITS.

The chief consideration with articles in this line is, that they should be as fresh as possible, and free from vermin and traces of vermin. Worms in dried fruits are never in sight, even though they may swarm below the surface. DRIED APPLES should be light colored, plump and acid. Evaporated fruit (by the Alden process, etc.) is preferred to sun-dried. It is often bleached in the fumes of sulphurous acid, which has a tendency to keep the fruit free from worms, and does not injure the flavor. DRIED PEACHES should be pealed, clear and dark. DRIED PLUMS should be pitted, clear and bright. DRIED BERRIES—the chief danger is from worms.

Raisins.

Raisins are dried grapes. The finest are the Dehesa "Layers;" next are the CLUSTER, or BUNCH raisins, and the "LOOSE," which are without stems. They are better in proportion to the number of crowns in the brand, as 1, 2, 3, 4, 5 Crowns. The small seed-less raisins are called "SULTANA," and come from Smyrna. VA-LENCIAS are the common cooking raisins. CALIFORNIA RAISINS (Muscatel) are excellent, very fast growing in popular favor, and are the coming summer raisin. The best raisins are of the "Last crop." Age tends to crystalize the grape sugar in raisins, and they are also liable to the attacks of vermin.

DRIED CURRANTS are the small dried grapes of the Ionian Islands. The "Vostizza" come in cases, and are considered better in proportion as they are larger in size. There are a number of varieties of currants. They should be bright and clean.

FIGS are said to be easier of digestion than any other dried sweet fruit, and are slightly laxative. "Eleme," signifies superior, or hand picked. Generally the last crop "Layers" (as distinguished from those in kegs) are the best; they should be fresh, moist, thin skinned, semi-transparent, and free from vermin. There are many varieties, and they are put up in all sorts of packages.

PRUNES are dried plums, or "French plums," as they are sometimes called. They are extensively raised in the valley of the Loire, in France; also in Germany, and about Bosnia, in Turkey. California prunes are also excellent, and very popular wherever they are known. The largest and freshest prunes are the best. They come in bottles, tins, bags, boxes and casks.

DATES.—This "Bread of the Desert" is the sun-dried fruit of the date palm, and is both nourishing and palatable. Dates were formerly packed in frails, but now come usually in boxes. Among the best varieties of Persian and Egyptian dates are the "Hallowee" and the "*Sair;*" some are large, yellow, moist, and little wrinkled, others are smaller, dark in color, with small pits; some are very sweet and insipid, and others almost aromatic in flavor.

TAMARINDS are the pods of a tree, growing in the East and West Indies, gathered when ripe, and preserved in sugar or molasses. They are acid, pleasant, healthful, and cooling. They come in bottles, stone jars and kegs.

NUTS.

ALMONDS are of two kinds, the sweet and bitter; the latter are only used for making extracts. Among the edible varieties are the Tarragona, Valencia, "Jordan," a corruption of *Jardin* (garden), etc. There are hard, soft, and "paper shell" almonds, and almond meats freed from their shells. FILBERTS are cultivated hazel nuts and come mainly from Sicily. PECANS come from Texas. WALNUTS from Italy, France, and Chili. BRAZIL NUTS grow along the Amazon in clusters on high trees. They are oily and rich. PEANUTS come from Virginia, and CHESTNUTS from Italy and our own Northern States.

TOBACCO.

The active principle of tobacco is the alkaloid nicotine, but it cannot be said that the effects of tobacco are solely due to this substance, for some varieties, as the Syrian, etc., contains little or no nicotine, yet are considered strong. The quantity of nicotine varies much in tobacco, or from one-half of one per cent. to eight per cent. As a rule, the finer the quality and flavor, the less nicotine the tobacco contains.

There are many varieties of tobacco, as those of Virginia, Kentucky, Maryland, etc., which are used mainly for chewing, while the Cuban, Turkish, Connecticut, Sumatra, etc., are considered better for cigars. All these tobaccos may vary again in species, as, for instance, there are the Orinoco, Cienfuegos, White Stem, One Sucker, Isabella, White Barley, Fiji Orinoco, Cubani, and many others. Havana or Cuban tobacco has long held the palm over all the world for making the most exquisitely flavored cigars. The aromatic principles on which its value depends can only be developed under a warm, moist climate.

Chewing Tobacco

Is used both in the "PLUG" form and as "FINE CUT," and in some localities preference is given to the one, while little of the other is sold. The New England and some of the Western States take their chewing tobacco largely in plugs, while the Middle States take more kindly to the fine cut. Detroit has a national reputation for the manufacture of fine cut tobaccos, which are extensively sold in tin foil and paper packages, and in bulk, in pails, etc. There are many hundreds of brands of chewing tobacco, both plug and fine cut. Some are the natural leaf, while others are sweetened; so that the most diversified tastes may be satisfied.

Smoking Tobacco.

North Carolina, Virginia, and Kentucky are foremost among the States in the manufacture of the smoking tobaccos, which are almost infinite in variety and sold in all sorts of packages. Among them are the "Long" and "Short cut," "Navy Clippings," "Granu lated," "Nigger Head," "Sweet Spun Roll," "Golden Cavendish," "Durham," "Fruits and Flowers," "Seal of North Carolina," "Seal of Virginia," and many others, besides imported varieties, as Persian, Latakia, Havana, etc. In addition to smoking tobaccos, many grocers keep a full assortment of PIPES, from the common clay up, through all kinds of briar and applewood pipes to the genuine meerschaum goods of every style and quality.

Cigars.

The value of a cigar depends not only on the quality of the leaf, but largely also on the mode of manufacture. If rolled too hard or too loosely, it will burn badly.

Why a Cigar Should Burn Well.

The best burning leaves must be used for wraps; if not, the air has no access to the inside burning parts, and the empyreumatical substances are volatilized without being decomposed. Such cigars make much smoke and smell disagreeably. If the cigar burns well, more of the nicotine is consumed and decomposed. Cigars, therefore, which contain little nicotine and burn poorly, are more narcotic in their effects than well burning cigars which contain a greater quantity of nicotine. Hence, the leaves of the Connecticut or "Seed leaf" tobacco, which burn freely and well, are much used for wrappers for cigars filled with Havana tobacco. Within recent years, however, the handsome leaved Sumatra tobacco is quite largely used for wrappers upon medium priced cigars, as it burns better than Cuban tobacco.

Quality of Cigars.

The real excellence of a very high-priced cigar is not in proportion to its cost, which depends largely on its size and the fancy of the buyer. For instance, a 50-cent cigar will burn no better nor be much, if any more fragrant than a 25-cent cigar. It may be larger, and the large Havana leaves, free from veins and suitable for use as wrappers for fine, large cigars are so scarce and high, as to enhance their cost out of all proportion to that of an equally well flavored, though smaller cigar. In fact, 10 or 15 cents should procure as good a medium sized cigar as average people care to smoke. The dude's dollar cigar is not much, if any better, except as fancy makes it so.

Many of the 5-cent cigars sold so extensively, contain a large proportion of Havana tobacco, and make a fairly fragrant and pleasant smoke. It is said that there are upwards of 100,000 open and proprietary brands of cigars on the market.

Cigarettes.—The sale of these little paper tubes filled with tobacco, has grown enormously within a few years and is still increasing. It is whispered that the ladies even, sometimes seek to find in them a whiff of the solace and comfort their brothers and husbands find in the pipe or cigar. There are many favorite brands on the market.

SNUFF.—This article which is made from the stems and refuse of the tobacco, or largely so, is comparatively little used in this country ; but in some sections, and especially in the South it is sold to a considerable extent. It comes in bulk and in jars, bottles, bladders, and packets. Among the varieties are " Carolina Sweet " and plain Scotch Snuff, Maccaboy and coarse French Rappee, scented or plain.

SOAP.

Soap is made by boiling down oils or fats in a water solution of caustic soda or potash. Through the acid properties of the fats, the oleine, stearine, margarine, etc., which they contain, combine with the alkali to produce the saponified compound.

Hard soap is made with soda; soft soap with potash. The more oleine in the fat, the softer the soap; the more stearine the harder. Rosin is also largely used, sometimes to the extent of one-third the weight of the soap. It increases its hardness, makes it dissolve easier in water and forms a more copious lather.

The Most Economical Soap.

Soap may be two-thirds water and still remain solid. Even dry, hard soap contains 20 or 25 per cent. of moisture. An excess of water causes soap to waste or dissolve too freely in use; hence, as soap is perpetually losing water by evaporation, the most economical to buy is that with some age and moderately dry, yet not so much dried that it will not dissolve readily and make a good lather or suds.

Effects of Strong Soap on Fabrics.

Soap must not be strong enough to injure fabrics or discharge colors, yet sufficiently powerful to render grease and dirt soluble, so that it may be washed away in water. Rosin soap hardens the fibers of wool, and alkalies, if used to excess, shrink woolen fabrics.

Hard water, or that containing lime or magnesia, more or less decomposes soap, and it floats on the surface as a greasy scum. But if an oily film rises to the top of soft water, it shows that the fat in the soap is not all saponified. Soft water is better than hard for fabrics.

What Soaps Are Made Of.

COMMON YELLOW BAR SOAP contains soda with fat and rosin. WHITE SOAP consists of tallow and soda. CASTILE SOAP is made of olive oil and soda. COMMON FANCY SOAPS are mainly ordinary soap colored and scented. Real BROWN WINDSOR SOAP is made of goat tallow, olive oil and soda. TRANSPARENT SOAPS are those which have been dissolved in alcohol. FINE TOILET SOAPS are made with as little alkali as possible, of almond, palm or olive oil, suet, lard, etc., colored and perfumed.

SHAVING SOAPS and CREAMS are made either with soda or potash, of fine tallow or cocoanut oil, which has the property of making a strong lather. MOTTLED SOAPS owe their variegations of color to the use of iron oxides. It is said that these cannot be effectively applied if the soap contains an excess of water, and that more skill is required to make good blue mottled soap than any other. The more any soap is worked over, or remelted, cooled, etc., the better it becomes.

A Wide Range of Choice.

There is a great variety of soaps upon the market, and language has been ransacked to find appropriate names for them. Among them are "FAMILY," "LAUNDRY," "IVORY," "BEST SOAP," "ELECTRIC," "OZONE," "BORAX," "SAND SOAP," "SILVER SOAP," "SAPOLIO," etc., and many scouring and detergent articles, as "PEARLINE," "SOAPINE," "SCOURENE," "WASHING COMPOUND," "WASHING CRYSTAL," etc.

In Toilet Soaps there is an equally wide range of choice, embracing every color and variegation of color, and every perfume that is agreeable to the smell. Soaps are also charged with disinfecting substances, as carbolic acid, etc., and variously medicated with sulphur, camphor, glycerine, and other materials for softening and healing the skin.

STARCH.

Laundry starch is mostly made from corn. The grain is crushed and fermented to a degree, when the starch is washed out and allowed to settle in large vats. The best qualities are washed and settled again and again; the number of washings grading the strength, purity and cost. Potato starch is more costly than corn starch, and, as it gives a softer finish to fabrics, is chiefly used by manufacturers. Corn starch for culinary purposes is thoroughly washed, purified and deodorized. Laundry starch should never be eaten.

The best laundry starch is in large, hard, flinty crystals; such indicate a stronger starch, containing less moisture than that with small or soft crystals. Laundry starch comes in bulk or boxes, and in paper packages. There are many fancy proprietary brands of starch, as "IVORY," "IVORINE," "GLOSS," "SATIN GLOSS," "SILVER GLOSS," "GLOSS POLISH," "ELASTIC," etc. Some of them are powdered, and contain borax, wax, or gum, etc., and are scented with winter-green, etc. Such come higher than the better grades of laundry starch in crystals, but it is a question if they are proportionately superior for family use. STARCH POLISHES, are preparations of spermaceti, wax, or paraffine.

Blueing (Laundry).

This article may be had in balls, powders, or in a liquid form. There are a goodly number of proprietary brands, some of which give a tint which appears somewhat greenish when placed by the side of a pure and delicate blue. The coloring principle is usually indigo, Prussian blue, or the favorite ultramarine. The most satisfactory laundry blueing is that which is really and intensely blue in tint, and which is most completely soluble in water, so that it will be well distributed and not make the clothes look streaked.

Candles.

In some sections, candles form an important article of trade. They are now made in a great variety of exquisite tints by the use of analine colors of various sizes and weights, and with patent self-fitting ends. The more costly kinds are made of spermaceti,

wax, stearine, paraffine, etc., down to the pressed, adamantine,
and common tallow candles.   Some carry embossed and handsome
decalcomania decorations and are either white, blue, green, pink,
yellow, red, etc., or assorted.   There are "BOUDOIR," "PIANO,"
"CLEOPATRA," "CABLE," and "FLAG" candles, wax "NIGHT
LIGHTS," "CHRISTMAS TREE CANDLES," and wax "GAS
LIGHTERS," warranted not to drip.

BRUSHES.—No domestic article is in more common use than the
brush in its various forms.   The best bristles come from the wild
hog of Russia and Poland.   The whitest and finest are used for
paint, tooth, hat, hair, and clothes brushes.   Some brushes are
made with one tuft only, like the paint brush, others with many.
The best are "Wire drawn;" that is, the tufts are bent double to
form loops through which wires are passed, to draw and hold them
firmly into the holes of the base.   Others have the tufts wedged
or glued in.   Brushes are made with long and short handles,
and of every conceivable form and quality, from "Sink scrubs"
upward.

BROOMS.—The finer the corn the better the broom.   A natural
green color indicates toughness and flexibility, and such corn is
better than that which is of a sickly yellow or lemon color.   But
the latter is often given the desired green tint by artificial colorings.   Plain or unpainted handles are best.   good brooms weigh
25 to 30 pounds to the dozen, but extra large and heavy ones are
made weighing 40 to 50 pounds.

WASHBOARDS.—There are fifty or more varieties of these "Mon-
day Morning Pianos."   Metal scrubbers are preferred to wood,
which is liable to splinter, wound the fingers, and tear the clothes.
And a plain crimp is better for fabrics than a rougher crimp, although the latter may extract the dirt quicker.   A favorite variety
have adjustable chest protectors.   CLOTHES PINS are of two kinds,
the old fashioned and the spring clasp.   The latter are little used.

MOPS.—There are two kinds in the stores; one of twisted twine,
which is generally thought to be most durable, the other of cotton and less expensive.

STOVE POLISH.—This is chiefly plumbago or black lead. Among the favorite brands are "DIXON," "RISING SUN," "A. B. C.," etc. There is also a liquid preparation or "Enamel," said to give a good polish without dust or smell, and with little labor.

BLACKING.—The best is that which will, without injury to the leather, most easily and quickly give a handsome and durable polish. Besides the excellent domestic varieties, there are the French Marcerou, and Jacquot's, in tin boxes, which are reliable and but little more expensive, and the old time Day & Martin's blacking in stone jugs. For ladies' use there are many domestic and imported SHOE DRESSINGS in liquid form, which require no rubbing.

MATCHES.—Common sulphur matches are made both square and round, and come packed in various kinds of boxes and papers. PARLOR MATCHES, of American, Swedish, and other foreign manufacture, are made without sulphur; and chloride of potash, antimony, etc., are often used instead of phosphorus. The splints are sometimes soaked in oil or paraffine to make them burn freely. SAFETY MATCHES have the phosphorus on sand paper and the other materials on the ends of the splints, and neither can be ignited except by friction with the other. There are many kinds of WAX TAPERS, "FLAMING LIGHTS," etc.

SEEDS.—The raising of seeds has become a large industry. Leading producers make careful tests of all their seeds, and even offer valuable prizes for the best vegetables and flowers grown from them. Some grocers lay in every season a fresh and full supply of all the seeds used in the garden or field, and they are almost always reliable.

BIRDSEED, FOOD, ETC.—Canary seed comes both in bulk and pound packages, either alone or mixed with millet, German rape seed, etc.; many packages contain a piece of cuttle fish bone. There are BIRD GRAVEL, BIRD PEPPER, MOCKING BIRD FOOD in bottles, etc.

INSECT POWDER.—There are a number of these vegetable preparations which are effective, if genuine and unadulterated, as the PERSIAN, BUHACH (or Californian), DALMATIAN, etc.

DISINFECTANTS.—Chloride of Lime in various sized packages of tin and paper, and various liquid preparations in bottles and kegs, are put up for domestic use.

PAILS.—Ordinary water pails have either 2 or 3 hoops. Those not painted on the inside are preferred. Wood pulp pails give good satisfaction, and a new pail with sunken hoops is just coming into market.

Grocers' Sundries.

Among other articles sometimes kept by the grocer, may be mentioned: Irish Moss, Anatto and other butter colorings, Licorice, Chewing Gum, Fruit Juices, Hops, Rennet, Ink, Paper and Pens, Pencils, Slates, Mucilage, Playing Cards, Beeswax, Cement, Concentrated Potash, Lye, Lime, Chalk, Oils, Kerosene, Dyes, Paints dry and mixed; Rosin, Tar, Turpentine, White Lead, Varnishes, Indigo, Glue, Putty, Powder, Shot, Caps, Wads, Axle Grease, Curry Combs, Condition Powders, Can Openers, Cordage, Coffee Mills, Bath Brick, Polishing Powder, Wick, Baskets, Boxes in Nests, Tubs, Dippers, Measures, Lemon Squeezers, Mouse Traps, Seives, Feather Dusters, Rolling Pins, Ax Handles, Tacks, Crockery, Glass and Stone Ware,

Borax, Bay Rum, Ammonia, Sponges, Camphor, Sal Soda, Perfumes, Plasters, Fly Killer Paper, Witch Hazel, and a great variety of standard drugs and proprietary medicines.

WINES AND LIQUORS.

While there are some grocers who, for various reasons do not handle these products, there are also many who keep for the family use of their customers a full line of choice wines, malt beverages, and distilled liquors. This work would therefore be incomplete without reference to these articles, and it is believed that the few facts given below concerning them will be found interesting and instructive.

WINES.

Pure wine is merely grape juice fermented. When the sugar of the grape is wholly or nearly converted by fermentation into natural vinous spirits or alcohol, the result is a STILL or DRY WINE. If the sugar is very abundant, as in overripe grapes, and a considerable portion of it remains unfermented, a SWEET WINE like Tokay or Malmsey is produced. When fermentation has proceeded to a certain stage and the liquid is bottled, so that it continues to ferment and produce carbonic acid gas, the result is an effervescent wine, as SPARKLING CHAMPAGNE. If, during fermentation, the process be arrested by the addition of alcohol, certain vegetable substances are retained in the liquid, and such wines as PORT and SHERRY are the product.

Composition of Wines.

Wines, as well as all varieties of malt and spirituous liquors, owe their intoxicating qualities to alcohol. But the medical and dietetic qualities of wine are not solely due to it; a mixture of water and alcohol, or whiskey of equal strength, has a very different effect on the animal economy. Pure wines contain also natural acids, sugar, ethers, albumen, phosphates, etc. Their value is, however, mainly determined by their "Bouquet" or flavor, produced by substances natural to the grapes, heightened and rendered more delicate by fermentation,

Alcohol and Acids in Wine.

The quantity of alcohol in natural wine from grapes, varies between 5 and 12 per cent.; the quantity of free acid from 3 to 7 per cent. If more of the latter be present, the wine tastes excessively sour, and is less easily digested; but some acid in wine is essential, and contributes much to its flavor and virtues. Besides the natural acids which exist in the juice of the grape, cheap and inferior wines often contain, also, the hurtful acids of spoiling, showing the approach to vinegar.

WINES OF THE WORLD.

France.

Even a bird's-eye glance at the wines of the world, might easily fill a volume. There are the superb French wines of Burgundy and Champagne, which ancient Provinces are now almost one splendid, continuous vineyard; and the Clarets, Sauternes, etc. of Bordeaux and Lauguedoc. Medoc and Haut Medoc are known to wine lovers everywhere, for here are the famous vineyards of the Chateau Lafitte, owned by Baron Rothschild; the Chateaux Margeaux, Latour, and many others.

The Wines of Germany.

The principal wine districts of Germany are the valleys of the Rhine and Moselle and their tributaries, whence come the well-known Hock and the red and white wines, which, though sometimes rather thin and deficient in flavor, are never colored, plastered, boiled, or have spirits added to them, and are therefore natural and wholesome. Here also is the renowned Johannisberg Castle vineyard, owned by the family of Prince Meternich. Every bottle of this wine bears his family arms, and it is the beverage of Emperors and Kings. By reason of its exquisite "Bouquet" it is pronounced "The finest and costliest drink on earth."

Wines of Hungary, Italy, Spain, etc.

Hungary sends forth her "Imperial" opal-tinted Tokay wines, made of overripe grapes, from which the juices are never squeezed but allowed to drop; other Hungarian wines are as dry as those of France, as mellow as those of Germany, and more fragrant than the choicest of Spain. Italy, Spain and Portugal produce wines of much repute, but neither of the latter two countries make sparkling wines; they supply Sherry and Port which generally have spirits added to them.

American Wines.

The wines of California and other sections of the United States are rapidly rising in popular estimation, and the time is probably not far distant when they will rival those of any part of the world. The consumption of domestic vintages increases with the constant improvement in their quality, which follows the slowly acquired knowledge, as to the best methods of turning the luscious juices of our own abundant grapes into wine.

Champagne.

The French make four varieties of champagne, viz.: Non-Mous-SEUX, CREMANT, MOUSSEUX, and GRAND-MOUSSEUX. The first is fully fermented wine, fined, drawn into bottles, and allowed to rest a long time. CREMANT is moderately sparkling. MOUSSEUX throws out its cork with an audible report and begins gently to overflow. GRAND-MOUSSEUX pops out the cork with a loud noise and overflows with much foam, as it has the pressure of five atmospheres. A sound, rather dry champagne is said to be one of the best of remedies for impaired digestion.

Good and Poor Champagne.

Good champagne throws up for a long time after being opened a continuous stream of small, sparkling bubbles of gas:

"Each sunset ray, that mixed by chance
With the wine's diamond, showed
How sunbeams may be taught to dance."

Even after hours of exposure, when it has lost all its excess of carbonic acid, good champagne still retains the characteristic flavor of true wine, while an inferior sparkling wine becomes, after exposure, almost as insipid as a mixture of sugar and water. The best are made from the first pressings of the grape. Those made from a third, fourth or fifth pressing require the addition of sugar and are cloying and far inferior in flavor. Imitation champagnes are made by sweetening any ordinary still wines or cider and charging them with carbonic acid gas.

MALT LIQUORS.

Malt liquors, properly so called, should be made only of malted barley, hops, yeast and water, but other materials are also used. PORTER is a beer of a high percentage of alcohol and made from malt dried at a high temperature, which gives it its dark color. ALE is pale beer with considerable alcohol and made of pale malt, with more hop extract than porter.

As every per cent. of sugar in the malt yields by fermentation about half a per cent. of alcohol, it is evident that ale, porter, and lager beer are stronger or weaker, as more or less malt is used in making them.

ALCOHOL IN BEERS.

BEERS are stimulating from their alcohol and refreshing from their carbonic acid, besides being tonic and somewhat nutritive. The oil of the hops gives them aroma and the lupulin they contain soothes the nerves. Their taste is vinous, sweetish, and bitter at the same time. The quantity of alcohol in malt liquors was given by Prof. Englehardt, as the result of analyses made for the N. Y. State Board of Health, in 1885, as follows.

		Per cent of alcohol by weight.
Lager, average	192 samples	3.754
Ale "	199 samples	4.622
Porter "	70 samples	4.462
Weiss Beer "	28 samples	2.356

Beer Adulterations.

It has been popularly supposed that beer is much adulterated. But the result of many analyses made by Mr. C. A. Crampton, for the Department of Agriculture at Washington, last year, show him "That beer is as free from adulteration as most other articles of consumption, and more so than some." The analyst found that, practically, no foreign bitters other than hops were used; but he also found that nearly one quarter of the samples analyzed contained, as a preservative, the unwholsome salicylic acid. This powerful drug is also largely used in the manufacture of cheap wines, etc., and the practice should be rigidly prohibited.

GINGER ALE is made by fermenting sweetened water, to which extract of ginger has been added, to such a degree as to generate carbonic acid gas and become effervescent. It is a heathful and agreeable beverage, containing some alcohol and being slightly stimulant.

GOOD CIDER contains 3 to 5 per cent. of alcohol. It is made from the fermented juice of apples. Many grown people acquired their fondness for cider on the "Old Farm" in childhood. It is sold by grocers in bulk, and is also bottled extensively and sold as "Champagne cider," and quite often as champagne.

DISTILLED LIQUORS.

The disagreeable taste of freshly distilled ardent spirits is due to the presence of fusil oil and other empyreumatic substances, which time alone can transform into harmless ethers which smell and taste agreeably, and produce an exhilaration over and above that of the alcohol which holds them in solution. Spirits can be distilled from any vegetable matter which will yield alcohol, yet many substances yield only a rasping, nauseous or flavorless liquor, which age does not improve. To some of these products, artificial flavors and color are given and the imitation articles are thus placed on the market. But true whiskey, brandy, etc., have a specific and original flavor of their own, and contain vegetable oils and acids.

Alcohol in Liquors.

The following table shows the proportion of alcohol (by volume) in the various liquors.

	Volume of Alcohol, per cent.
Cognac Brandy	55 to 70
Arrack, made from Rice	60 to 61
Whiskey, American	60
" Scotch	50 to 51
" Irish	50
Rum	49—7
Gin	47—8

BRANDY.—This is made from wine ; that from white grapes is preferred and it requires about seven bottles of wine to make one of brandy. Even the best Cogñac is burning and rough until kept for two or three years, and it improves with increased age, until, when thirty or forty years old, it develops a flavor somewhat similar to that of vanilla.

WHISKEY is a spirit distilled either from fermented malt, rye, barley, oats, wheat or corn. The very best and sweetest grain is only used for making good whiskey. American whiskey is more easily obtained pure than perhaps any spirituous liquor and is therefore more reliable in this country. The name whiskey is a corruption of the Erse and Irish word *Usquebaugh*, "Water of Life," the French *Eau de Vie.*

RUM is made from distilled molasses and skimmings from the boiling sugar.

GIN is distilled from unmalted grain, the product being rectified and flavored with juniper berries.

Favorite Brands.

CHAMPAGNES come in quarts and pints, *Sec* or "Dry," "Extra Dry," etc. Among favorite Brands are those of Heidseick, Mumm, Roederer, Cliquot, Bouché, Morizet, Pommery, Delbeck, etc.; the AMERICAN Champagnes of California, Urbanna, Pleasant Valley, etc., besides various imitation sparkling wines. Among favorite CLARETS are St. Julien, Medoc, St. Emillion, St. Estephe, Floirac, Pontet Canet, Chateaux Margaux, Lafitte, La Rose, etc.; also the SAUTERNES and WHITE WINES of Graves; Barsac, Chateaux, Yquem, Latour, etc. There are the Johannisberger, Hockheimer, Rudescheimer, Marcobrunner of the RHINE; the ITALIEN Capri, Falerno and Chianti; Port, Sherry and Madeira of various brands; and Claret, Port, Sherry, Muscatel, Angelica, Tokay, and other vintages of AMERICAN MAKE.

CORDIALS include Anisette, Benedictine, Curaçoa, Chartreuse, Maraschino, Kirchwasser, Kummel, Chocolat, Ginger, Raspberry, Rock and Rye, and Absynthe. There are Ales, Porter, Stout, Lager Beer, Peach and Apple cider, Orgeat, Soda and Sarsaparilla. Favorite Brandies are those of Otard, Hennessy, Martelle, Robin, Seignette, Dupin, and good California Brandy; also Blackberry, Cherry, Ginger, Peach and Cider Brandies. Besides scores of fine AMERICAN WHISKEYS, there are the SCOTCH Thistle and IRISH Cruiskeen Lawn; Old Tom, London, Holland and Geneva GINS; St. Croix, Jamaica and N. E. RUMS. Many Grocers keep also a supply of NATURAL and ARTIFICIAL MINERAL WATERS, as the Congress, Hathorn, etc., of Saratoga; Carlsbad, Seltzer, Clysmic, Vichy, Apollonaris, Williams Quelle, Lithia, Hunyadi; and a ariety of Bitter Waters.